This book is dedicated to
Brandon's mother, Yvonne Mably.

KAFFE FASSETT IN THE STUDIO

A fabric collage of my large florals, cut and applied to a patterned background with fusible web.

KAFFE FASSETT
IN THE STUDIO

Behind the Scenes
with a Master Colorist

KAFFE FASSETT

PHOTOGRAPHS BY DEBBIE PATTERSON

ABRAMS | NEW YORK

INTRODUCTION 7

PART ONE
Studio and Home Life

PART TWO
Studio Work

PART THREE
How To

Introduction

In my lectures and workshops, participants often ask about my house: can they visit? I have to discourage this—I'd never have time to do my work if I had to entertain visitors! So, I thought I would write a book that attempts to show my creative spaces and processes. This book aims to satisfy that curiosity about the flow of color that comes from inside my house.

I started my adult life with the firm conviction that I was going to be a serious fine artist. The plan was to paint whenever I could and convince galleries and buyers to show and consume my work, affording me a living. When I first moved to London, I didn't find this too difficult. With the optimism and energy of youth, I painted or drew most days and attended dinner parties and country house weekends. I met enough people to keep a stream of them visiting the studio with the occasional buyer. London was cheaper in those days, so the sale of one painting could pay my rent for a month and keep me in the humble café food and groceries I'd cultivated as a sustainable lifestyle. I usually dressed in charity shop or flea market finds, so expenses were definitely controlled. The sale of a painting a month or a commission to illustrate a book or magazine article could keep me going.

After a while, the socializing and charming of potential customers was getting harder to sustain and doubts about whether I was good enough as a painter, an affliction that affects most artists from time to time, started making this lifestyle more arduous for me. There were days when I could not find inspiration to motivate my creative projects. Paintings took up room to store, they were a problem to ship to galleries and overseas customers, and framing was expensive.

Then, I discovered textile making: first knitting, then needlepoint, and eventually patchwork. Each of these was a way to create pools of color that became a very visceral part of one's life as opposed to paintings that were just hung on walls. Textiles could wrap around you, be sat on, cover you cozily in bed or when watching TV, and—the biggest bonus for me—I discovered I loved the process of creating a textile. I was motivated every step of the way. Knitting always fascinated me—how the two needles and colored yarns created this magic web. And needlepoint was a simple way to create more complex images. I found I could make bags, slippers, and belts as well as cushions. But, for me, the best of all of these was patchwork. To create designs quickly from squares of colored fabric was an instant thrill. I also started creating my own prints that I could share with a world market. All textile making is just another way to play with color that is at the same time deeply therapeutic to do.

I don't think there is ever a day when I can't face making a textile. The hard thing for me is to leave my studio and go out to lecture, teach, or break off to write something like this! To sit at the end of my studio, surrounded by yarn or piles of fabric, and dream up a new design is what satisfies my soul. BBC Radio 4 keeps me informed and amused while I contentedly while away the hours, spinning some magic new combination of colors into existence.

So, color has become my subject and the motivating factor for watching TV and films, traveling, and—best of all—collecting good examples of color usage in vintage textiles and pottery.

MY COLOR LAB

Obsessed as I am by color's power, I often call my house a "color lab," yet I'd never label myself a color expert. Color is such a gigantic enigma, changing and revealing different possibilities each time one concentrates on it for more than a moment. The average person, particularly in Western cultures, seems to rank color quite low on their list of significant priorities, which accounts for the predominance of grays and beiges in fashion and neutral preferences in interiors. That said, the pale, neutral world of sea-washed stones, weathered wood, and graying hair does have an intense beauty to which I'm often drawn.

People who have overcome their nervousness of using color, and begun to perceive its inherent ability to enhance lives, tap into my fascination with it. To them, I don't need to explain why it is so high on my list of priorities. The people I've come across who really "get" me often are those who work with color.

I remember meeting a tall man in a wallpaper factory who was mixing a huge vat of yellow paint to be used on one of my designs. He was standing over a container three feet deep with gallons of paint and needed to adjust the yellow color from lemon to a slightly dustier tone. Taking a stick, he dipped it into a small can of black paint and dropped a few dribbles into the sea of bright yellow. After a stir, he saw that a depth had entered the yellow,

Looking from the painting studio through to the landing. A drooping collage of flowers on the door was for a bag printed for QuiltMania in France.

knocking the brilliant edge off it. I was so impressed at his casual handling of the stick. I knew from experience how easy it would have been to ruin many gallons of expensive paint.

"How did you know how much to use?" I asked. "Did you train professionally?"

"No," he replied. "I just watched my father, who had this job before me."

Gardeners often seem to tune in to the range of tones of the plant world, be they bright or subtle. A good flower arranger is a true artist, in my opinion. I'm inevitably struck by the small arrangements I've come across in India and Bali—picante mixtures of shapes and colored blooms that linger in my mind as a painting does. When a garden is planted by a sensitive eye and you catch it in its prime season, it is one of the most life-enhancing experiences. The older I get, the more I'm in awe of the natural world in all its seasons. Blushes of wildflowers on a hillside in spring can thrill even the most neutral fashionista, but even winter, with its almost ghostly hued remains of flowers and grasses drained of their bright vitality, can have a delicate beauty.

I've learned from the natural world that shades of a color, when placed together, have a certain complex glow. Watching a rose mature makes me aware of so many close shades that make up its intense impression. When I go to a natural-history museum and behold the brilliant colors of minerals, I notice the color is never just a single shade: pure lemon, lavender, and pink minerals are intensified by multiple tones. Good stage designers use this technique, too. A production of the Peking Opera that stays in my mind was a scene done entirely in many shades of yellow with touches of lavender, sky blue, and candy pink. There were no dark or muddy colors to break the saturated lemony spell. Even though contrast adds a jazzy excitement to colors, if you want them to really glow, then closer tones help enormously.

I often limit my range of color tones, so that a group of deep, dark colors, or only pastel tones, can enhance each other. Saying that, proportion has a large part to play in the impact of a color. A large field of scarlet or magenta surrounded by small bits of "kick" colors can impress the socks off your audience. Maybe a bright red can be added to spark a pastel palette. Sometimes my best ideas come from seeing very kitsch uses of colors and pattern as I travel—markets, cheap store displays, circuses, and amusement parks can offer surprising clashes of color that can come in handy when you want to spice up a quilt or an exhibition.

Back in the fifties, as a young fledgling artist in New York, I spotted an ad for ketchup. The photographer had laid a large table with many white plates, bowls, and cups, then placed the bright red bottle off to the side. I was so surprised by the gleaming white arrangement that I started painting nothing but white and neutral crockery on white tables. It was a study of highlights and shadows that lasted for some years, before I came to England and discovered the deliciously patterned world of oriental and Indian paintings. The pattern-on-pattern that became all the rage in hippy fashion at the time became the subject matter for my still lives. All this pattern, of course, used a lot of color, and I was hooked!

Ever since that time in the late sixties, I've been fascinated by the different patterns and color palettes mingling together in cultures—particularly the Japanese, Africans, and Roma, who have always delighted me with their fearless playing with pattern. It's one of the things that drew me to patchwork—a world of mixed pattern in the scrappy quilts I favor.

In my knitting, I love doing stripes or dots, or rows of flowers and geometric motifs. One of the things about patterned knitting is the pace you can achieve, because each section of a pattern knitted spurs you on to the next section of the design. I don't know how the plain, one-color knitters ever get a project done! I did a beige sweater once and I nearly lost the will to live. I never knew how much I'd done, and the unfinished section seemed endless. I'm known as a fast knitter, and it's mainly down to the motivation of pattern.

With that love of pattern in mind, I have created strong patterns in the knits in this book that should keep you knitters motivated to keep going. They are easy-to-memorize motifs that repeat with exciting color variations to prevent the works from being predictable. I'll start you off, but I hope that each knitter adds their own variations to make each work more of their own personal vision in the end.

Part One

STUDIO AND HOME LIFE

History of the London House and Studio

When I first moved to England, I was able to find a wonderful two-room studio with a balcony in Lansdowne Crescent, in London's Notting Hill area. That was a rental and it served me well for my first few years. It was near one of the best flea markets in London at the time, with weekend stalls selling fruit, vegetables, and all manner of secondhand items, including vintage clothes, pottery, textiles, tools, and so on. During the week, I dipped into the hundreds of more legitimate antique shops that lined the Portobello Road. As my income gradually improved, I was able to shop for more valuable pieces to add to my still lifes.

When an artist friend came to visit London from New York and needed a cheap place to rent, I searched London until I located a second-floor flat in Kilburn (which at the time seemed quite far out of the center of London). She was a single mum and also needed room to paint and sew to earn her living, so this whole floor in an Edwardian house was a good deal for her. When I found the flat, it had an ugly 1950s carpet of brilliant colors on a dark background that we called the "swirls of vomit" style. The living room was furnished with two leather-bound seats from a sports car—comfy enough but low to the ground. When she married an Englishman a year later, I was given first refusal on the flat and jumped at it because it was bigger than my two-room place in Notting Hill.

I took over the flat, sold the car seats and carpet, and established my own look, seeing the place mostly as a work base. There was a small kitchen next to a tiny cramped bathroom, and a bedroom at the back end of the flat. The large front room with a fireplace was my living room, with a small extra bedroom next to it. I used the hall as a library to store most of my books. The back bedroom became a place to sleep as well as a painting studio. Two

A shot taken years ago. Marks & Spencer used the needlepoint tapestry for Christmas packaging one year. The rug is made of rags—hooking was an obsession at that time.

large windows gave a gorgeous light onto a table against the wall that housed whatever still life I was working on at the time.

I lived on that one floor for some time, paying rent to an agent of an absent landlord. One day, the agent came to visit and noticed that I had filing cabinets in the flat. The next thing I knew, I was taken to court with an eviction notice. The judge asked what evidence there was that Mr. Fassett was running a business from the flat. "Your Honor, he has filing cabinets in the property!" His Honor considered the rest of the proposal and spotted an error in the documents. "Your case is invalid because of this error." "Couldn't you just overlook that, your Honor?" "My dear man, this a court of LAW! Pay Mr. Fassett's expenses and remove yourselves." I went home amazed that I hadn't been turfed out, and, because I could see they were stuck with me, I offered to buy the building. I was duly sold it at a bargain price.

A few years later, as I could afford it, I bought out the tenants on the bottom and top floors and found myself in possession of an entire house in London! I had no central heating, but would collect scraps of wood on my many walks around the area—often a broken chair, off-cuts, or a packing crate would supply enough wood to warm me up when burned in my fireplace. I had an old rickety table in the hall that served as a sawhorse to cut wood for the fire. When people visiting were really cold, I'd ask them to cut some wood for the fire—I found that warmed them up as much as burning the wood did. Being a casual sort about tidiness, the sawdust that got trampled about the place didn't really bother me.

When I met Brandon Mably in 1990 (see also page 93) and invited him to come share my house, everything about the house changed. By then, I had bought the upstairs and downstairs, so properly occupied the three-and-a-half floors. Brandon was amazed that I had only a few old rugs and chairs—usually things I'd found in junk shops or on the streets. "You need a sofa and a proper carpet to cover the whole living room floor." So, we went sofa shopping—very grown up for me! Once that was in and I'd bought a handsome carpet, we looked and felt a lot more civilized.

I found these Dresden plate blocks at the Houston Quilt Festival one year and created a quilt with Liza Prior Lucy that blends so deliciously with my patterned plates. Needlepoint cushions sit on a sofa covered in early Designers' Guild roses of mine.

THE WORK STUDIO

The Big Studio at the front of the house is where I paint out the artwork for my patchwork prints. Large shelves house our latest collections of current prints to be used in the next book of patchworks we publish every fall. There is a flannel "work wall" near the cutting table. After using my cutting board and rotary cutter to cut out pieces of a new design for a quilt, I can lay it all out on the flannel wall that holds the pieces in place—that way I can stand back and see how the arrangement looks.

I usually sit in a corner near the large windows, knitting or doing my needlepoint designs. I have a low Afghani chair that brings me close to the piles of yarn I accumulate on the floor. I will also sit and sew, by hand, the blocks I make for patchworks, putting them up on my design wall to see how they "read."

My knitted swatches are made from collections of yarns I gather to use. First, they are Rowan Yarns, as I develop designs for their knitting books each season. I'll put all the colors of Felted Tweed, perhaps, in a basket and start my swatch for a new design. If the original colors don't work, I'll add to the basket what's needed. Sometimes I use Peruvian yarns that are sent by Peruvian Connection. I do two collections of knit designs for them each year. The box of yarns they send me are always gorgeous dusky shades of alpaca and pima cotton dyed to their Peruvian palette.

The studio always has several projects going on at once, so my yarn collection and swatches are always around me. I'll also have a patchwork idea on the go, so stocks of fabrics are spread out on the carpeted floor to see how a color theme emerges for a quilt. As design work is quite intense and I lose concentration at times, I usually have a jigsaw puzzle in progress on one side of the studio to give me a little light relief.

TOP RIGHT: Brandon and me listening to a radio play and stitching floral panels for Ehrman Tapestry. BOTTOM LEFT: Placing pot shapes on a block of the month I designed for an Australian magazine with Kathy Doughty of Material Obsession. BOTTOM RIGHT: My work wall gets a real workout with knit ideas and patchwork using my shot cottons.

My work wall is so useful, here trying out two proposed patchworks of knitted swatches.
Bold geometry in jewel tones and stark contrasts seems to obsess me at present.

Just some of the books and magazines on decorative arts that give me
endless inspiration. Brandon's desk is beyond the door.

OPPOSITE, TOP: A collection of my ribbons so beautifully woven by Renaissance Ribbons. OPPOSITE, BOTTOM: Me picking which hand-woven fabrics to include in my new shot cotton range. Such a hard choice! ABOVE: Brandon and me working in the studio. Brandon is stitching his cushion design Stars, and I am starting to paint my Tiddlywinks design for a patchwork print.

THE PAINTING STUDIO

Opposite the Big Studio is my little painting studio. It's also a storage place for my china collection and the artwork that Philip Jacobs, Brandon, and I produce twice a year. The top of the artwork drawers (a substantial plan chest) serves as a platform for any still life I plan to paint.

Since I don't do that much easel painting these days, this room becomes a catchall for storing rolls of paper and canvas, boxes, and stuff that needs sorting at a later date. The light, when I do paint, is not even the northern light that is recommended for artists, but rather a western light that I find full of life until about midafternoon when it shines too viciously into the room, forcing me to hang veils to soften the glare.

LEFT: Here I am wearing a shirt I had made from one of my batik prints. The red chair I found on the street, but it remains a favorite. ABOVE: Some would wonder how I could paint in this chaotic jumble of a studio—a good thing it doesn't faze me. The studio is a storage room for my china, shells, paints, and rolls of paper, as well as the ongoing artwork drawers.

A Syrian embroidery in pink on a Kelly green background is the base of this still life. I love the singing green, turquoise, and yellow pots on this bold cloth.

THE LIVING ROOM

After seeing and admiring other rooms in the world that had oversized flowers for decoration, I painted large rose clusters on the living room wall (see the following page). At first, they sat on the beige background I'd painted some years before. When a group of Japanese visitors was due, I suddenly felt that the neutral ground looked a little sad, so I quickly did a rough wash of warm yellow behind the roses. I liked the effect, although I'm not sure if the businessmen noticed.

Later, Tricia Guild came to commission me to do a fabric collection for her and loved the walls. She wanted me to do the same effect for a furnishing fabric—it was quite a success when it was launched.

For a few years, I lived with large white cupboards at the far end of the room that were used to house my patchworks. Brandon begged me to paint something on them to make them more part of the room. So, one day, I plucked up the energy, went down with my paints and some good blue-and-white porcelain references, to paint a number of those cupboard doors (opposite). At first, the effect was too glaringly bright, so I glazed over them until they softened to the right level of faded glory.

At the far end of the room, under the windows, I keep my ever-growing collection of needlepoint cushions. To the side of the windows is my couch, under a large Chinese ancestral portrait. I bought this painting of someone's ancestors from an antique shop. It was so big I had to take it off the stretchers and have a local frame shop remount it for me in the room, where it has lived ever since. It's one of my favorite possessions. A television sits across from the couch, which Brandon and I watch most evenings when we're home.

Our television sits behind the daisy scarf. I found the maroon carpet with lime yellow leaves and flowers in Australia. The needlepoint chair was stitched by Brandon's sister, Eleanor, among others. The painted roses on the wall inspired a Designers' Guild collection.

The patchwork storage cupboards I painted with images of blue and white pots, a collection of which sits on top of the cupboard to the left.

ABOVE: Some of the ever-growing piles of patchwork quilts, with a crocheted throw by Rosy Wilks.
OPPOSITE, CLOCKWISE FROM BOTTOM LEFT: My favorite oriental pot. Needlepoints of the
same pot sitting on the sofa in front of the ancestral portrait. A mosaic apple. My rose fabric design
for Designers' Guild that was inspired by the wall painting in my living room.

Some of my needlepoint cushions surrounding my oriental jars and porcelain Buddhas.

THE DINING ROOM

When I put together my *Glorious Interiors* book in 1995, I did several dramatic set-piece rooms specially for the book. The dining room was the most ambitious. At the time, I had just met Karen Beauchamp, who ran a wallpaper company. Among other designs, she did a Sanderson vintage panorama of Kew Gardens, which came in shades of gray, sepia, and autumnal tones. She donated them to me for a mention in the book. I quite cavalierly ordered a few sets of each colorway so I could collage them to create a tapestry-like effect in the large room. She supplied them without comment, and we went to work, carefully cutting around each tree to collage them together. When it was all hung, I inquired how much each set was going to cost the average customer—I was shocked at how extravagant I had been! We asked Karen to lunch and she was delighted that something so original had been done with her designs. I was able to find a large machine-made tapestry to cover my dining table, which created the perfect effect to complement the walls. At an auction, I found a good oriental carpet to complete the rich patterned feel of the room. It is quite beautiful in candlelight for our occasional dinner parties.

LEFT: A cabbage teapot made by Roger Michelle sits on my dining room mantelpiece.
ABOVE: The leaf dining room is a perfect setting for an old-fashioned Christmas party.

When I dreamed up this dining room, I wanted to celebrate the beauty of leaves. The wallpaper is a view of Kew Gardens in three different colorways superimposed on one another. The knitted throw and cushions depict leaves, as does the needlepoint chair, cushions, and slippers on the table. A red cabbage is the subject of the rag rug under the couch. A tapestry of trees covers the table, with pottery in leafy themes.

THE UPSTAIRS KITCHEN

I first painted this sunny kitchen Kermit-the-Frog green—it was so bilious we could hardly go in it, let alone cook or sit there, so I repainted it the soft yellow it has remained to this day. This room is much used, first to cook our meals, lovingly prepared by Brandon, then to sit there eating, chatting, and doing crossword puzzles (one of my passions). When I come in for lunch, I'll often pin up a needlepoint, swatch of knitting, or painted fabric colorway at the end of the kitchen to see how it hits me from a distance.

I was much happier once I painted the images of pots of flowers on the cupboard doors, added porcelain handles from Australia, and put up a few blue-and-white plates. I keep a shelf here for my pots and flower vases—and I like seeing my cups all dancing on hooks above the kitchen table.

Brandon and I did the mosaic behind the sink in mostly white and neutral shades with odd patterned pieces added in. It's pleasing to contemplate as you wash up (we have never graduated to a dishwasher).

ABOVE: The fridge magnets are all paintings of fruit and veg boxes by Jane Martin.
LEFT: My sunny yellow kitchen with its collection of china. The plates on the table were designed by Brandon and me. The still life of mugs is by Peter Plamondon.

ABOVE: The delicate palette of this mosaic behind my sink is good to contemplate when doing the washing up. OPPOSITE, CLOCKWISE FROM TOP RIGHT: One of my still lifes on the landing. My kitchen cupboard doors are painted with blue and white pottery. A Christmas card from the Missoni family is the perfect backdrop for my drippy glaze jug.

THE BATHROOM

The ceramics of Rupert Spira (see also page 129) were exactly the look I was after for my bathroom—his tiles line the floor and washstand. This is in fact my most realized room in the house—I always feel the rest of the place is in a state of flux, about to be turned into a set for one or other of our books. In addition to the tiles, I've collected many of Rupert's beautiful bowls and created a shelf here for my collection, so I could see them every day. The bold red-and-green striped sink was made from one of his punch bowls.

The many plants always seem to bring a cool element that fills the corner nicely as I gaze in the mirror. The wall color took a long time to decide on. I had Rupert's tiles put in, then, looking at the wide range of tones they came in, I settled on a golden ochre tone that was in several of them. It made the best background color for both the tiles and the antique painted chest I'd bought in a shop up the road. I store some of my antique quilt finds in this chest.

LEFT: My sister, Holly, didn't start painting until she was in her late forties. This quick study of the coast was a masterwork in my eyes and reminds me every day of the Big Sur coastline I was raised on. OPPOSITE: The basin that Rupert Spira made for me out of a punch bowl. I love the red and green bold stripes. The tall red vase and green bowl are his as well.

LEFT: When I shopped for tiles made by Rupert Spira, I picked the ones that had gone "wrong." These rejects with their uneven colors made my bathroom floor such a rich combination of hues. The painted chest I found in an antiques store goes so well with them. The painting sitting on the chest is a student effort by my great-grandmother. CENTER: Pots by Rupert Spira on shelves.
RIGHT: The mosaic treatment of the window surround is also on the table.

My still life of the pots that live on my sink: a ginger jar and Rupert Spira pottery and tiles.
The small purple vase I found in a museum shop in Charlotte, North Carolina.

THE NEUTRAL DOMAIN

The back of the ground floor has become Brandon's neutral domain. He put up my early white-on-white paintings and installed off-white couches, rugs, and curtains. His bathroom is lined with a white mosaic, mostly the remains of dishes of which I had used only a bit of pattern for a more colorful mosaic. I used blue/white, pink/white, and black/white transferware for the border around the sink. It was interesting to do such a restrained mosaic after our highly patterned and colorful ones.

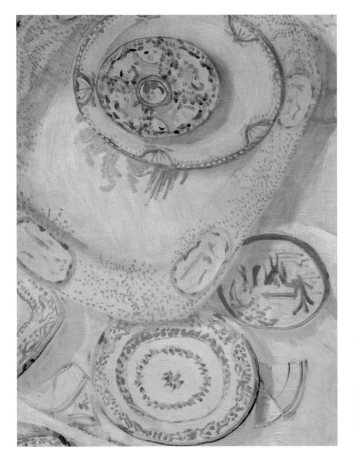

OPPOSITE: An early still life of white and neutral-colored pots I found in Portobello Market. LEFT: A detail of the painting on pages 70-71. The first signs of my love affair with English and oriental china.

Brandon enjoying his suntrap back terrace and garden. The soothing palette of creamy pale tones expands the light from his skylight.

The white and neutral mosaic in Brandon's bathroom has borders of toile pottery. Someone once commented that the bathroom ceiling made her feel as if she was underneath a glass dining table.

One of my early still lifes. You can see that my pure white-on-white arrangement is being invaded by pattern and a plate of shells and pebbles. It was my transition into full-color still lifes.

TRANSITION SPACES

Noticing that the front door had a very rigid few rows of glass squares in a sort of checkerboard pattern, I designed an effect of tumbling glass panes and had it made by an artist friend. Karen Beauchamp donated the oriental wallpaper in chalky pastels in the hall, and I carpeted the floor and stairs with antique carpets found in flea markets. Between exhibitions, we keep our lushly needlepointed high-back chair in the lower hall.

The stained-glass windows were designed and made by John Fitzmaurice. We both liked the idea of the ordered checkerboard at the top of the windows tumbling in a chaotic fall.

The grand vegetable chair that is so at home against the oriental wallpaper. The chair took me and my crew of three stitchers three months to complete.

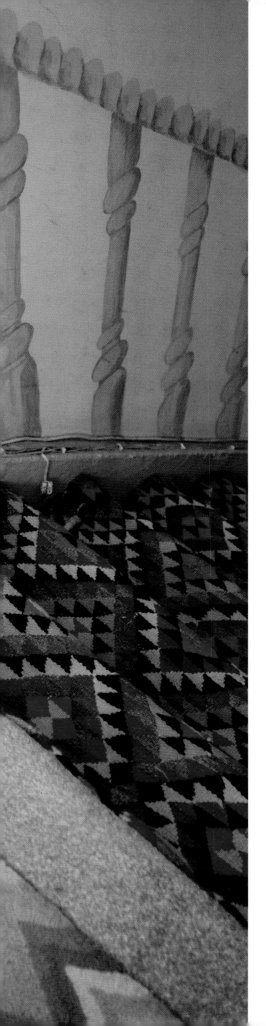

LEFT A self-portrait of me with a beard. CENTER: Jill Gordon painted my faux handrail on the stairs. RIGHT: My vegetable carpet against my wallpaper produced by the Designers' Guild.

My hall "library." I suppose most people would have tidied their bookshelves before photography, but here for all to see is my collection of china, beaded and mosaiced items, even painted eggs. The poster is of a Bill Gibb outfit with my knitted vest; it was the 1970 Garment of the Year at the Costume Museum in Bath.

ABOVE: My china pieces seem to crop up everywhere, even in the library. I enjoy looking at the masks and Peruvian hat as much I do all the art books I collect. RIGHT: We try to keep yardage of all of my fabric prints, but as you can see from the stacks on the floor, it is a bit like King Canute fighting the waves.

OUTDOORS

Outside, we laid a multitoned patio and covered the walls in a bright tile mosaic. Noticing that I had little time to garden, Brandon has taken it under his wing. He hired an artist gardener friend, Hannah Sindall, to keep it in shape. They worked out a succulent garden on top of the tool shed so we could view it from the kitchen window on the third floor. I'm always grateful for the color and varied foliage of the garden in all seasons as I return home from our travels.

OPPOSITE: The back garden is such a delight to look down on from the upstairs kitchen. The shed roof is planted with succulents. RIGHT: A window box that matches the mood of the plants.

CENTER and ABOVE: In the front garden, inspecting my Kaffe Fassett roses.
FAR LEFT: A striped Rosamundi cluster contrasts excitingly with my batik shirt.

My tiled and mosaiced garden terrace outside Brandon's quarters.

OPPOSITE, CLOCKWISE FROM TOP LEFT: The mosaic panel of hollyhocks at my front door. Brandon's wellington boots, on which I painted a Tumbling Blocks pattern, blending nicely with our terrace tiles. Brandon's mosaic of colorful diamonds in the porch always attracts attention. ABOVE: A mosaiced window box with perfectly toning plants.

People

Like many artists trying to forge a different path through a given discipline, I became a control freak. When I tried to get my first book on knitting published, I was fought by the art director and editor, who were bent on producing a typical knitting manual. When my photographer and I insisted we wanted double-page spreads and images bled to the edge of the pages for my colorful garments in his stunning settings, the editor cried, "You are creating a coffee-table book!" Well, duh!

But that was only one of the fights I had along my path, so it was a great relief for me to find creative souls I could trust to help me realize my vision. In fact, without the energy certain people have generously allotted me, I could never have achieved what I have. Learning to trust the intelligence and imagination of others not only has been liberating for me, but definitely makes me less of a lone wolf.

Liza Prior Lucy and me in front of our Oriental Pots quilt.

BRANDON MABLY

When I first established a design studio in this house, I was definitely a one-man band. I hired a small group of people to help knit and stitch needlepoint projects for me. I only possessed one floor of the house in those early days, and most of the work was done in my bedroom with a kerosene heater to keep us warm in the winter. Those were days of intense stitching and knitting in that cozy room: two of us sitting cross-legged on the bed; two on chairs; piles of yarn in the center of the carpet; and the radio informing us of the latest poetry, plays, and interviews, which had us all in a listening mood most of the time. I would also man the phone, talking to journalists and planning travel to do workshops, as well as dreaming up designs to keep everyone working creatively. Then, I would break off at midday and cook lunch. I did get to the point where someone else was responsible for the phone, and we took turns cooking lunch, but I was definitely feeling the strain.

I met Brandon by chance—he was living nearby and took an immediate interest in all the projects we were working on in the studio. He was working as a chef then, but spent every spare moment sitting in a corner of the studio, drawing and learning to stitch and knit. By then, I'd bought and occupied the whole house, so we all spent most of our time in the upstairs studio. One day, Brandon said, "I'll cook for you so you can keep working." Then, he observed that projects in the studio took a long time to complete, making commissions very expensive, and that he and I as a team could get more done without having to manage other helpers. I gave him the job of running the studio, and we started collaborating. Although he had no art education and a certain level of dyslexia, he had a brilliant eye for a good design and—most special of all—a real color sense that matched my own.

My house was furnished in a very "bare necessity" sort of way, which Brandon was quietly skeptical about. He noticed I had carpets rolled up and not used, so he got those out and warmed up the floors. Then, he encouraged me to get a decent sofa (a very novel idea to me!). He hung up paintings and encouraged me to paint the walls and my storage cupboards. The effect was astounding. As civilization dawned on my surroundings, I found my mood lightening.

At that time, I'd started to feel a bit world weary, having traveled all over Britain and Europe giving workshops and lectures. One day, I got a call from Australia asking me to

do a workshop tour. I said I'd do it but needed an assistant (thinking to myself—Brandon hasn't been there and I'd love to see his reaction to that landscape). When they agreed to fly Brandon over, a new chapter opened for both of us. In the next decade, we did tours of America, Canada, Europe, Iceland, China, Japan, South Africa, and India. That travel, with its profound stimulation in exotic sights as well as the encouragement we got from sharing our creative secrets with others, added a depth to our lives. Back in the studio, after every trip, we found ideas flowing from all the sketches, photos, and bits of design (in the form of material patches, patterned objects, and the odd quilt top) that we'd brought back.

OPPOSITE: Brandon's collection of scarves, hats, and travel finds on his screens and shelves. The crocheted scarf at top right is by Sophie Digard, a favorite of us both. LEFT: A small oil painting of the Virgin Mary is a Peruvian treasure that Brandon has pinned to his painted screen.

PHILIP JACOBS

Philip Jacobs is the third artist in the Kaffe Fassett Collective, along with Brandon and me. A very classical artist, Philip paints out his designs from a large archive of antique prints. Old French and English florals or Japanese references often inspire his prints.

I met Philip years ago and was amazed when he told me he designed furnishing prints. He had a strong, athletic build, better suited—in my imagination—to a builder or rugby player. When I showed curiosity in his work, he came to my house and gave me a slideshow of his prints. I was blown away: big, generous floral prints, exquisitely depicted.

After several viewings of his work, I invited him to join the Collective. I was delighted that he had a vast archive of source material, including French and English wallpapers and vintage furnishing fabrics, which meant he could furnish me with endless classic, detailed florals that are so useful to contemporary quilt makers. As we developed a good working relationship and he saw that his furnishing-style prints were eagerly being purchased by quilt-makers the world over, he set to exploring other inspiration sources, such as images from Asia.

The very first collection of his that I accepted marked the beginning of our collaboration. Philip said, "I'll do the rendering of the designs, putting them into repeat, but you, Kaffe, do the colorways." I was thrilled, as that is what I love to do—to take a handsomely depicted print idea, done in generic colors, and transform it. For starters, I will flood the background with an unexpected color. I also love depicting blooms and foliage in surprising colors that I feel sure will add spice to the quilter's cannon.

Philip visits my studio one afternoon each year and opens a huge portfolio bursting with new ideas for me to choose from for our next season. Within the selection, he always includes designs that I've turned down on past occasions, and he is so right to do so, as I often chose one or two for a present collection that I'd passed over before. Certain designs have a right and wrong time to launch. I pick six designs for each collection and then set about the task of painting them out in my own colors. When it comes to colors, I always try to give our fans a good basic paint box; in other words, a good blue, red, pastel, and grayish version of whatever print is being launched.

Philip has inspired a huge following on social media, something he well deserves for his consistent discovery of new print subject matter and his gorgeous rendering of those classic images. When the fashion house Coach chose the Kaffe Fassett Collective as their muse for their fall 2019 collection, it was Philip's big blooms that featured heavily.

LIZA LUCY AND COLLABORATORS

One of the things I love about textile making is the collaborative nature of it, and a particularly vital collaboration is with the expert knitters and sewers who work with me to create the pieces that end up in my books. First was a stunning knitter who came to my studio to pick up helpful hints on how to start her own career in knit design. I wasn't at all sure that I could help this tall, slightly aloof beauty when she came to work with me. I handed her a very complex knit I had done as a commission and asked her to look through my vast stash of yarns and reproduce a second version of the jacket. She spent a long time digging out the colors and weights of yarn needed and went home to try to knit something similar. A week later, she was on my doorstep with a finished garment. When I compared hers to mine, I could hardly tell which was which, even though she had had to make several changes because she couldn't find all of the hundreds of tones I'd used in my knit. I was blown away and of course had to work with her. She was fast and more efficient at beautifully finishing each piece than I was, and also had an instinct that helped her work out any fashion shape we needed. Her name was Zoe Hunt and later became Zoe Dewe-Mathews. Zoe worked with me on several books and collaborated on many commissions to clothe Hollywood ladies in unique knitwear.

Brandon and me at a gallery opening with quilt sewers Mary-Jane Hutchinson, Janet Haigh, Julie Harvey, and Ilaria Padovani.

When my first book, *Glorious Knitting*, came out in America, it caught the attention of a yarn rep who bought six copies for her friends and family. That very night, she got a call from a yarn company she had never heard of, asking her to rep for them. She initially refused, saying she had quite enough companies to rep for, but was then told that the yarns were for this new book by Kaffe Fassett. "Damn! I could have had those books wholesale!" she said to herself. Liza Prior Lucy became a brilliant rep for Rowan Yarns and, because so few people got my name right, coined the phrase "You've got a safe asset with Kaffe Fassett."

Liza had a baby for whom she was making a quilt and decided that I would be good at the craft. She wrote to me, suggesting I start designing patchwork. I wrote back that I was snowed under working on a needlepoint book and finishing up a mural commission—that was me politely saying "no." However, Liza heard "maybe." She started to send me blocks of patchwork based on my knit designs, and I started saying things like, "That one is okay, but too much white." She shot back with, "See! You are designing!"

I finally gave in and visited her in Pennsylvania to start making quilts for our first book, *Glorious Patchwork*. We drove to every fabric shop in her area and I noticed that small-scale prints ruled. I had noticed that the vintage and antique quilts I loved had dynamic large-scale prints in them, more akin to the scale of furnishing fabrics. So, I started designing my own large-scale prints. First, a Swiss chard print, then large roses and cabbages. These made the Thimbleberry (a hugely popular small-scale print company) crowd tremble in their boots! Liza encouraged me to do more and sewed up all the quilts for our books with the help of a talented group of quilters she found in her area. Later, she opened one of the biggest online shops from her home that she had extended for that purpose. Since that fortunate meeting with Liza, I've coauthored several hardback books with her, and she, Brandon, and I are in constant contact as we advise our fabric company and publishers to produce and promote our creative ideas.

As Liza was so far away, I looked for a second collaborator in England with whom I could produce quilts for my annual patchwork and quilting books. Pauline Smith became indispensable, and my trips to her studio/home in Yorkshire became deliciously creative times. We'd set aside three or more days each year to create twenty quilts for the next book. She would have all the fabrics sent to her, ready for us to cut up and use in layouts I'd create, usually using a few combined antique quilt ideas. Every evening, we'd eat delicious meals that Pauline drummed up. She and her husband also shared my love of jigsaws, so we often had one on the go.

Nothing seemed to faze Pauline, and we spent many happy hours dreaming up and sewing new patchworks. When the quilts were done, she would record all the instructions and edit each book, so it was a huge blow when she was forced to retire from quilt making. Unfortunately, Pauline developed asthma from the fibers stirred up by cutting and sewing fabric, so she had to stop all textile work. I was devastated, but fortunately was put in the capable hands of Janet Haigh, who ran a studio of sewers near Bristol. That became another brilliant collaboration, as we continued to create new ideas for the annual collection of prints coming in.

A big part of the answer to the question of how I get so much done is these amazing collaborations with very creative souls. Janet will often fill in some left-out detail or suggest a good substitute for a fabric that is no longer available, which shows me she gets my message!

Another fascinating collaboration is with my niece Erin, whom I paint with on my yearly visit home to California. We often paint the same still life of some of the objects I store at my sister's house in Big Sur. This annual painting spree led to a show in a local museum and a book that her husband, Tom Birmingham, produced in 2020. I realize that coming back to easel painting is a good, different way of playing with color. Erin tells me that she learns a lot from the objects I place on certain color backgrounds, as do I. Jumping from media to media gives anyone interested in the mysteries of color a fresh eye on the subject.

ABOVE LEFT: Richard Womersely weaving.

ABOVE RIGHT: Quilt sewers Julie and Ilaria being guided by Janet Haigh, who oversees the making of half the quilts for each of our quilting books.

PHOTOGRAPHERS

I started my career authoring textile books with the brilliant guidance of Steve Lovi. He was an artist-turned-photographer whom I met in California in the early sixties. He visited me in London when I first settled here, and lived in my studio when we went on one of my trips home to California. He was one of the few people who saw completely what I was about and was able to guide my work in a way that totally made sense to me.

When I had built up a body of knits, Steve saw at once that there was a book in it. He went with me to a few publishers, proposing the sort of book we envisaged. The dream we had was so different from any other knit book on the market that we were met by great resistance. We wanted a coffee-table book, similar to books on carpets or textiles that so many of my knits were inspired by.

Random Century finally took the bait, seeing the same possibility that we saw in these colorful textiles. Steve photographed the knits and did a brilliant job. It gave birth to my first big hit: *Glorious Knitting*. We went on to produce four more books, Steve producing more and more stunning photographs and, more important, directing me in what to design

LEFT: My brilliant friend, photographer Steve Lovi, keeps me entertained while I knit on our travels.

next. When he moved back to America in the nineties, I had to find a new photographer—a huge task after so many years of collaboration with a genius.

I looked listlessly through portfolios of prospective photographers. One day, a picture suddenly leapt from the pages. It was a small, chipped, blue enamel teapot sitting on a tray in a field of lavender, and on the tray were a few heads of garlic in a lavender mesh bag. All those cool shades of lavender and blue went straight to my heart, and I felt here was a photographer who saw color the way I did. Debbie Patterson was an attractive blonde who had trained as a lawyer but was now assistant to a fashionable female photographer. I hired her on the spot, and we started our amazing journey. We have now done countless books together as well as many articles in magazines.

Brandon and Debbie have a very similar sense of humor, so our trips around Britain and overseas became quite fun occasions—except for me sometimes panicking that we won't get our book finished in the two or three days we usually have designated. I've learned that we all click together and get amazing work done on schedule, so we proceed without too much stress. I often think of filmmakers who use the same crew in film after film, because they get to know each other and rise as a group to tackle the next challenge.

There is always a great rush of energy and excitement for Brandon and me as we do a recce for the next book. We might go to Portugal, Malta, or Italy to explore a location for its color and textural possibilities, armed with a contact sheet of the new collection of quilts to be included in the book. We spot a good background for each quilt, making a little scrawled note next to the photograph. That usually takes a day or two, then Debbie arrives and we lead her to all our spots. We hang or drape the quilts in their unique locale and have her shoot them. Sometimes the light is too bright during the day, meaning we have to start early in the morning and continue in the softer evening light. Luckily, we all have similar taste in food, so after an intense day's work, we seek out the best restaurants in the area and chill.

When the photographs arrive, we choose which ones best sum up the impression we had at the shoot. The art editor then does the first layout for the book. Probably the most important task on any book for us is going over and over the layout to be sure the book reflects our initial vision—whether a picture is cropped too tightly, or included in a multi-image collection, or bled to the page edge to give more impact—it makes or breaks a book for us.

Debbie Patterson photographing a quilt in this grand, muraled room at Port Eliot House in Cornwall. It featured in our book *Quilt Grandeur*.

Daily Life

My mind seems to gravitate toward the complex in most things: intricate patterns in textiles, still lifes crammed with objects when I paint, and lots of pattern- and color-mixing in my room decors, so a scattering of fabric, yarn, broken dishes, or paints does not upset my equilibrium. That doesn't mean I don't appreciate a well-ordered room. I'm always deeply affected by the calmness in my bedroom or studio after the cleaner leaves. I'm also very grateful that Brandon constantly makes order in our house!

OPPOSITE and LEFT: Painting my Fruit Mandala artwork that became a 108-inch wide backing fabric. I've always loved seeing how fruit is arranged in farmers' markets on our travels.

TIME AND MOTIVATION

After they have seen one of my lectures, people often ask me, "Do you ever sleep?" In a one-hour lecture I can show a great body of work, from mosaics to patchwork and all the other mediums I exercise, so it can look quite impressive. The thing is, I don't participate in so many of the things that eat up other people's time, when they could be creatively employed. I don't own a mobile phone, and I don't bother with computers (although, of course, they are vital to today's way of living, so I have a wonderful assistant, Bundle, and work hand-in-hand on everything with Brandon, who knows all about that tech stuff). I don't spend much time socializing, since I go out into the world each year to meet many thousands of people. For motivation I have my lovely radio, always tuned to plays and interesting interviews. And finally, I don't have a compulsive urge to tidy up—I'm quite happy in my chaotic mess as long as I can lay my hands on the colors I need to finish a design, or knit, or stitched piece, or patchwork. Brandon and Bundle do their best to keep order and always know where things are when I scream for them. Richard Womersley looks after all our accounts and contracts and keeps us sane with his daily visits. He has a weaving studio a few blocks away from us.

Another thing that is important to me is the F word—*focus*. Many people in our workshops used to chat, eat, fumble through their bags, and do anything but steadily get on with producing the quilt design they came to do. Brandon and I finally figured out that you need to give people in workshops time limits. "Everyone should have the first stage of the design done and in place by eleven o'clock!" Suddenly, classes where few got much done became powerhouses of productivity, and often the choices of color were better because they bypassed the analytical brain and worked more instinctively and intuitively. After most workshops, Brandon and I are amazed how many fresh ideas have been discovered, which is the highest reward to us as instructors.

TOP LEFT: A scene from the end of a day's workshop, somewhere in the world. The diamond quilt is very popular with students. BOTTOM LEFT: A painting workshop display board showing the postcards that inspired students' color choices on my Turkish Delight print.

TOP: The crowded mixed pond on Hampstead Heath. ABOVE LEFT: The men's pond on a quiet morning. ABOVE RIGHT: The mosaic fireplace I made with shards of old china found on my Hampstead Heath walks.

EXERCISE

Sitting working in my studio most days, I find that I need to balance that out with exercise. I'm just as prone to stiffness and apathy as most my age, but I've learned to shake myself up at the end of the day and walk to my gym to swim a couple of lengths of the pool or do some gentle rowing or muscle-building efforts. I figure the walk there—about two miles—is a good stretch for me. I also take two Pilates classes a week, which is a great balm to my aching muscles and boosts my balance. I don't drive a car, so I often walk to the places I need to go.

Once a year, I meet up with my sister Holly at Rancho La Puerta, a superb health farm in Baja, California. There, we walk several miles every morning, swim, do exercise classes, and eat gourmet organic food. One of the greatest things about it is the fascinating guests. Every evening, we sit at a mixed table for dinner and get to know several new strangers. Another wonderful aspect is the visiting speakers: experts in medicine, literature, diet, philosophy, and the arts. As a result, we experience a week each year that reinforces our health and stimulates our minds. We've been going every spring for the past eleven years.

In the 1990s, I was the subject of a TV series, *Glorious Colour*. Anne James, the director and producer of the series, would go outdoor swimming at Hampstead Ponds, even in winter. One fine summer day, she called me up: "I think it's time you started swimming on the Heath—I'll pick you up at seven tomorrow morning." That was the start of the most life-enhancing chapter of my life. For the next ten years or so, I was greeted by a beep from her car each morning. We would park on the opposite side of the heath from the ponds so we could get a good walk and would trek across the heath discussing the world, books, films, and life's lessons. I'd often spot shards of patterned china in the muddy earth. I considered these rare treasures from the past and would pick them up and take them home. I knew one day, when I had enough, I'd make a mosaic with them. That opportunity arrived when I needed to replace some ugly tiles in my living room fireplace. It was delicious to be able to gather these beautiful bits together in a place I could view every day. I made some Dutch-style tiles in blue and white to go with them. Now, every time I glance at the fire surround, I think of those fresh morning walks and long summer swims or winter dips in the ice-covered ponds and the engaging talks with Anne. There is something so profound about moving through outdoor water, surrounded by trees, especially when it's almost too cold for comfort. The afterglow I felt kept me almost entirely free of colds for that period of my life. I was so grateful to Anne for the experience that I bought a bench on the Heath, dedicated to her.

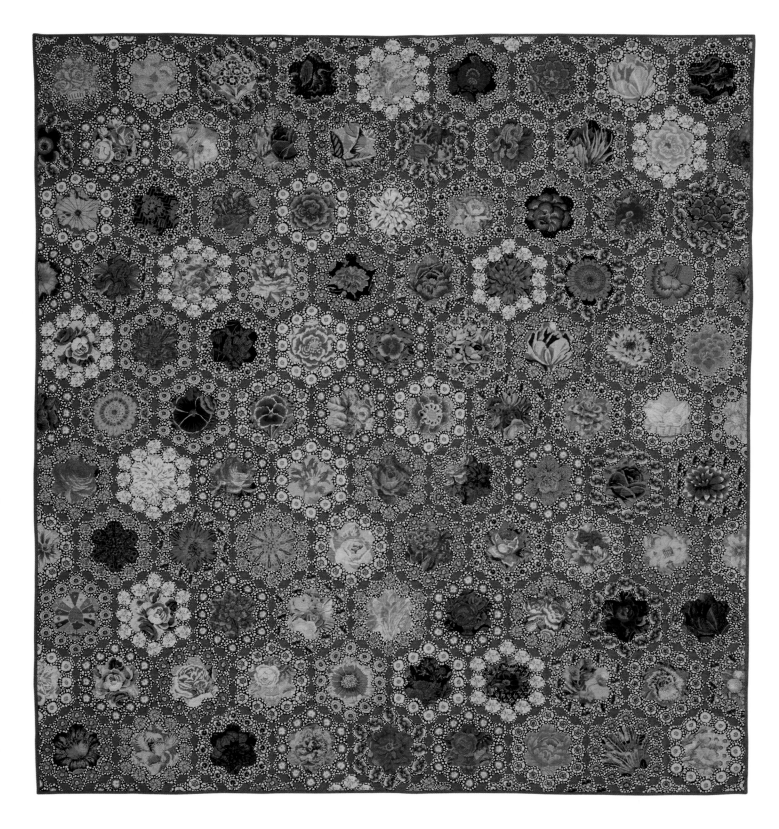

PUZZLES

What is it about puzzles that is so alluring to me? I suppose they relate to that part of my nature that loves complexity and making order out of a pile of raw materials. Brandon once explained me to someone, saying, "Kaffe is always solving puzzles." Whenever I start a jigsaw puzzle, I'm thrilled as each piece fits into place and the image starts to take form. If the work is by an artist, I gain insight into the brushwork and color balance of the artist in a deeper way than any other. If I'm having a tough time solving a visual design in textiles, or if I've been writing for too long, the puzzle table with its fragments that need to be joined together is irresistible and instantly releases any tensions that have built up.

At the end of each intense working day in the studio, I go for a walk to my local coffee shop, picking up a free newspaper on the way. In the warmth of the shop, with a cup of chai in my hand, I start working on a daily crossword puzzle called Codeword. Every letter has a number and one word is given to you—the solution to the puzzle comes to me quite quickly. If it doesn't, I tuck the half-done puzzle in my pocket to bring out over dinner or breakfast. I find some answers come more easily when I see it at a later time.

These puzzles definitely bring a welcome ritual to my life. Every now and then, some of my friends who are aware of my jigsaw obsession give me a custom-made puzzle depicting one of my quilts or a quilt made with the Kaffe Fassett Collective fabrics. I find it quite otherworldly to be piecing together something that I've created.

ABOVE LEFT and OPPOSITE: A custom-made puzzle of a quilt by Australian quilt-maker Kim McClain; the quilt itself was made from Kaffe Fassett Collective fabrics. It was bizarre piecing together fabrics that were so familiar to me. ABOVE RIGHT: One of my favorite painters, Giuseppe Arcimboldo, is the subject of this intriguing jigsaw puzzle.

BOOKS AND TRAVEL

When I'm traveling, one thing that always draws me in is a bookstore. For years, I was mostly attracted to pictorial books that could give me inspiration for my design work, so books on subjects as diverse as carpets, mosaics, interiors, fashion, art, and travel had me snapping up any volume that had at least two or three good ideas spotted at a thumb-through in the store. I knew I'd find much more when I could peruse the pages at leisure in my studio.

Lately—in the last eight years or so—I've become an avid reader of novels and biographies. I love to share a good book with my sister (who was always, from a young girl, an obsessive reader) and other good friends, such as Brandon's twin sister, Belinda, and Pauline Smith, who used to sew quilts with me. There is wonderful solace to be had from a good "visual book." An author who can conjure up the colors and physicality of a place has me enthralled.

I read slowly, savoring a good book for weeks. I find myself relating the insights in a book to everyday existence, adding quality to my life. So, my bookcases groan with reference books, decorative arts books, and magazines, as well as the good reads that I have not given away over the years. Our tube station has a free book exchange in the form of a shelf full of donated books. I'll take a bagful to those shelves every now and then, and have gathered several good reads there, too.

Whenever I spot a good picture book that has color and pattern, no matter what the subject is, I buy it as a spark to inspire further work. I am especially drawn to books on cultures vastly different from my own. Countries that celebrate their individuality and local flavors and colors are particularly intriguing.. Their fearless use of color and pattern moves and inspires me. Even a photograph of a shantytown, with blocks of color on a neutral base, can give you a good color scene for a muted aesthetic.

But there is no substitute for visiting a place in reality. While I was writing this book, I visited Cuba for the first time. Wow! I found it to be a treasure trove of the most creative and lush use of colors in completely unexpected combinations. Brandon and I walked every day, viewing this living museum. It is like a great sound stage designed by an inspired musician.

An African beaded skirt, a Peruvian knitted hat, a beaded bag, and a Japanese blue and white print are just part of the booty I have brought back from my travels.

We half expected a dance routine to break out—music and colorful people are everywhere, swaying to seductive rhythms in front of tall pastel- and jewel-colored houses with baroque doorways and balconies. For me, dress and shirt patterns in colors that harmonize or clash with a painted wall on a street makes people-watching take on quite a new dimension. One day, we will go back to shoot a book there, for sure. Until then, we are filled with courage to use colors with more lively abandon. Brandon and I both got the same buzz from travels in India, Africa, and Guatemala, too!

Of course, ideas come from so many sources. The fashions in a foreign place have such a different flavor, and the way a shop window display is staged can often spark a quilt layout or knit pattern. One of the areas of my library that gets used most is the section on vintage quilts. I refer to these often when I'm looking for a good layout to suit the new prints I have coming out. And the world of pottery is another good source of surface pattern ideas for knits and patchwork prints. I love looking at Chinese, Japanese, and Korean pots and porcelains—their playful use of pattern always gives me ideas.

So, you can begin to see how my collection of picture books on many subjects can be useful, while actual travel helps me to see more distinctly, because the sights are so fresh and new.

ABOVE LEFT: I search foreign markets for fabulous collections of pattern, such as these Islamic patterned bowls and tiles I found in Morocco. ABOVE RIGHT: A colorful temple that we found in India. OPPOSITE, TOP: Reference books in the studio with a new shipment of fabrics from the printers. OPPOSITE, BOTTOM: A wire basket from South Africa and the knitted cushion it inspired lie on a knitted bedcover.

A good example of the delicious color combinations to be found in Havana's Old Town.
Art murals are only a part of the colors of Cuba; the vintage cars also come in fabulously bright colors.

FASHION

I am often asked in interviews who my favorite fashion designer is. It's a hard question for me, because I really don't pay too much attention to the fashion world, except for a few outstanding mavericks.

One such was Alexander McQueen, who had the soul of a fearless artist. Brandon was so smitten with his show at the V&A Museum that, one morning, he took me there the minute it opened. We shared the magic theatrical experience with only two other people, so it was like a private view. Beautifully mounted, it was like *Alice in Wonderland*—presenting this inventive designer's work in that theatrical way with special lighting and dramatic music was just right. Bravo, V&A!

Before I discovered McQueen, my absolute favorite designer was the Frenchman Christian Lacroix. His wonderful mix of patterns and use of color were so close to my own at that time, and—boy—did he stand out in the corporate-turning eighties! I found a wonderful book on his environment and influences and spotted so many things I could definitely relate to: mosaic tables, crazy quilts, and most of all his richly patterned designs for women. *Pieces of Pattern* was its to-the-point name. I was so moved by it that I wrote him a fan letter. He wrote back telling me that my books were an influence on him! The only thing that slightly took the shine off this was that he addressed the letter to "Madame Fassett." (Oh well, when my first book came out in America, they changed the title from *Glorious Knitting* to *Glorious Knits* and everyone was on the hunt for the latest knit book by "Gloria Snitts"!) In fact, while I was working on this book, the editor came across a floral dress on a background of stripes by Lacroix, in the same vein as my quilt design on page 148, so I feel that he is definitely on the same wavelength as I am.

In September 2018, the famous fashion house Coach rang me up and asked if I minded being a muse for their design team. I was thrilled to be part of the fashion work, so I opened my archive of fabrics and finished quilts to them, to choose whatever they fancied. From the Kaffe Fassett Collective they chose quilts and fabrics heavily featuring Philip Jacobs's big florals, along with needlepoint ideas. They saturated the palette in wine and moss tones, using a lot of black, which made us look very sophisticated.

Part of a collection by Coach that used Kaffe Fassett Collective prints. Here you can see my Bold Blooms print (BOTTOM), a dress in my Jupiter design, and a patchwork interpretation on this coat.

RECURRING THEMES

As I cast an eye over my years of designing, I can see that I often seem to be on the tack of a theme, such as multiple flowers, white-on-white still lifes, and upscale, carpet-like themes in my knitwear. Just recently, I am very excited by bold stripes and sharp contrasts in my color work. One thing that has always fascinated me is to explore the same theme in different mediums: I find taking a geometric motif from a knit to a hooked rug to a mosaic to a needlepoint introduces scale and textural differences to the motif that are really stimulating.

Here I'm showing how the idea of high contrast can go from painting to patchwork to knitting to printed fabric. Also, how I see the theme demonstrated all over the place, such as in street performances or on buildings, or even deckchairs by the seaside. I feel it's as though the world is dishing up confirmation of my chosen theme as I go about my life.

OPPOSITE, TOP: Striped floral vases that so inspire me. OPPOSITE, BOTTOM: A recent painting of contrast bowls and vases on a blue and white cloth sits on a patchwork of multi stripes. ABOVE LEFT: My favorite street performer in his brilliantly painted stripes. ABOVE RIGHT: Brandon looking dangerous in a striped T-shirt that matches the painted stairs in Hastings.

ABOVE, CLOCKWISE FROM TOP: For years I specialized in smoldering close tones in my design work, but lately the boldness of high-contrast black and white, and jewel tones, seems to appeal more and more. Here are designs by Philip Jacobs and Brandon that I use in patchwork. On the outskirts of Havana is the magical suburb of "Fusterlandia" (in the Jaimanitas district), which is almost entirely mosaiced in fantasy patterns by the artist José Fuster. Here, a guide (just seen) dresses to match the contrasting dark and light of the mosaic. Brandon's crossword-inspired knit echoes that mood. RIGHT: Me displaying a high-contrast knitted patchwork in front of a quilt using every stripe I could find.

EXHIBITIONS

There is something very gratifying about having an exhibition of your own work. I've always had a fascination for theatrical presentations, so—for me—a good exhibition should give the viewer the feeling that they are experiencing a piece of theater. The colors and patterns in my work can appear either to be an indigestible jumble or as exciting pools of color and themes of pattern that do an intriguing dance.

When colors are grouped together, they enhance one another and create exciting vibrations. I feel the world of colors is very like the emotional experience of listening to music. A great exhibition should be like a symphony.

I've had the great honor to have museum shows all over the world. Each of them has been a different experience, mostly down to the curator and art director of each museum. One of the most significant and satisfying exhibitions I've had was staged by a talented opera designer, so it really was like a musical experience. It was designed by Johan Engels for the American Museum in Bath in 2014. Every section and color mood was perfectly orchestrated, and his most unique idea (of many) was to print my needlepoint and patchwork designs as floor coverings, so the colors and patterns completely surrounded you as you moved through the experience. Another good show was at the Fashion and Textile Museum in London in 2013, where Sue Timney used black-and-white columns to expand the museum space.

I would say the main plus of an artist having an exhibition is that we get to see our own work arranged excitingly and well lit, as opposed to seeing our work folded in drawers and cupboards, or stacked against the walls of our studios.

The exhibition of my textiles at the Fashion and Textile Museum in London, designed by Sue Timney, using classic black and white stripes.

My Collections

LAUGHING BUDDHAS

I began collecting these big jolly men with their small children climbing over them, as they reminded me of my childhood (my mother loved oriental art, and I would often see these Buddhas in the shops she frequented). They became a good luck symbol for me if I spotted one in an antique shop on my travels. I prefer the older ones that are so definitely hand-molded and glazed. I remember finding several beautiful old Buddhas on my first trip to Vietnam, but had to resist buying them, as government customs won't allow any antique china to leave the country. All the hotels there had gorgeous tempting collections of china in their lobbies that would be confiscated by customs as you left the country. I bought a beautiful blue and white bowl—it is held at customs for me to look at whenever I return there.

PORCELAIN AND POTTERY

When I first came to England, in 1964, I was steeped in my painting career. Because I could see at once that the mercurial weather was going to bar me from painting outdoors regularly, I made the decision to paint still lifes that would become my interior landscapes. To this end, I started collecting jugs, cups and saucers, plates, and bowls—all in shades of white. At that time I was on a white-on-white kick—color or pattern were far from my aesthetic.

After a while, I started visiting the V&A Museum in London regularly and saw how thrilling the pattern-on-colorful-pattern was in the Indian miniatures in their collections. I loved the way flower prints mixed with stripes, paisleys, and checks, and it led to a new approach to my paintings. I started collecting detailed cloth and china so I could emulate the same dance of pattern I saw in those charming paintings.

English flea markets and secondhand stores were awash with deliciously patterned china and tablecloths. I even found the odd patchwork quilt to use as a base for my still lifes. Flowery china, often chipped or broken, became my models as I arranged my theater of pattern. As I sold more paintings, I was able to afford pieces that were less damaged, and the patterns on the china and vintage cloth became subject matter for textile designs as well as objects in my still lifes. These pieces of china still delight me when I see them arranged on my shelves, or occasionally serving as a vase for flower arrangements.

I don't collect seriously, as many collectors do. The only contemporary potter I've paid attention to is Rupert Spira. I've watched him develop over the years since he was a teenager, as he started a pottery when he got his first kiln. Just as he started his studio, he was asked if he made tiles. He replied, "yes I do," then quickly had to figure out how he could actually make his first tiles. He made many "mistakes" with his first glazes, and these became my favorite items. I bought as many as I could at a reduced price and used them to line my bathroom floor and around my washstand (see also pages 56–63). I also had Rupert create my sink out of one of his punch bowls. I love the bold red and green stripes of the sink and take joy in it every time I brush my teeth, wash my face, or shave. I usually keep an arrangement of a Chinese ginger jar, one of Rupert's vases, and one of his beautifully patterned bowls at the corner of the sink, too—they wink at me each time I use the bathroom.

Shelves housing some of my smaller china pots, sorted by color.

ABOVE: A study I did of French coffee bowls I found in Morocco. OPPOSITE, CLOCKWISE FROM TOP: Pots stored in my kitchen often get used for flower arrangements. Shelves of contrasting pots. An original oriental cloisonné vase.

Some of the oriental pots that share my living room.

VINTAGE TEXTILES

Each October, I visit an annual quilt market in Houston, Texas, and catch up on all the new designs pouring into the patchwork world. There are always vendors selling antique quilts and patches of old prints. I buy a quilt or a block that catches my eye, especially if it is an intricate design I've never attempted or an arrangement I could use to show off my latest prints. Often, I'll buy just a quilt top, because actual quilting is not as interesting to me, and an un-backed, un-quilted top is easier to fit into my crowded luggage.

I also visit antique shops on my teaching tours and bring home prints on shawls, handkerchiefs, kimonos, or scraps of fabric that I can use to inspire further prints. I also use these prints and embroideries in my still life painting. I have two sets of drawers that house most of my smaller vintage textiles, such as scarves and tablecloths. The old quilts will be in trunks or on shelves.

OPPOSITE: A sample of my vintage fabric collection, with pieces from Japan, Russia, Syria, and an English needle-point. LEFT: An American beaded bag.

OPPOSITE: Boxes of vintage fabrics and (BOTTOM) a chest of drawers in my store cupboard, painted by Jill Gordon. ABOVE: A portrait I did of Tricia Guild and her daughter in the eighties. The bedcover, by Pat Fairchild, is the only contemporary quilt I live with.

Part Two

STUDIO WORK

Fabric Design

My patchwork projects usually start with the painting out of a textile print collection. My designs can come from many sources—a shirt noticed in a charity shop, an antique embroidery, a tiled or carpeted floor spotted on my travels and noted on the back of an envelope or in my diary, a wall painting, or—quite often—a fragment of pattern I'd seen in an old quilt that really spoke to me.

I hand-paint my print designs in gouache on paper about 16 inches (40 cm) square and have to keep track of each color I use so it can be reproduced by my very accurate printers in Korea. I draw out the idea in pencil first, making a grid at the bottom of the design to record the various colors I use.

As I paint, I keep putting the partial work up on the wall to see how it is reading from across the room. When I'm done, I print out a corner of the finished work and paint over each color in it to create a different colorway. It's always amazing to see how a delicate, pastel-rose print on a sky-blue background is transformed when rendered in dark tones against a black background. Essentially, I am supplying my followers with a paint box with which to create their own patchwork quilts, so I always try to give them a red mood, a blue mood, a dark mood, and a soft gray or pastel mood, so that any number of possible patchworks can be born.

Brandon will often be working alongside me or at the kitchen table painting his own designs. We often comment on each other's work, encouraging or gently criticizing something we feel doesn't hang together.

The drawers that hold all the Kaffe Collective artwork. Those lines of color chips help the printers to print a different colorway of each design.

Philip Jacobs, the third artist in the Kaffe Fassett Collection, also comes to me once a year and we go through a large portfolio of work he has prepared for me to choose from. He presents me with artwork in generic colors so that I can transform it into shades that enhance our collection. I pick six designs for each collection and then set about the task of painting them out in my own colors.

I await the day the fabrics return from the printer—sometimes a little different from my intention and I have to strengthen some colors, or soften them, or change a whole background from purple to emerald green. When they come back a second time, corrected, I sit down with the lovely new textile prints spread out before me and dream up a quilt layout that shows off the fabrics to best advantage.

Painting out my Hydrangea print by hand in gouache. I love the way the blooms emerge out of the patterned background.

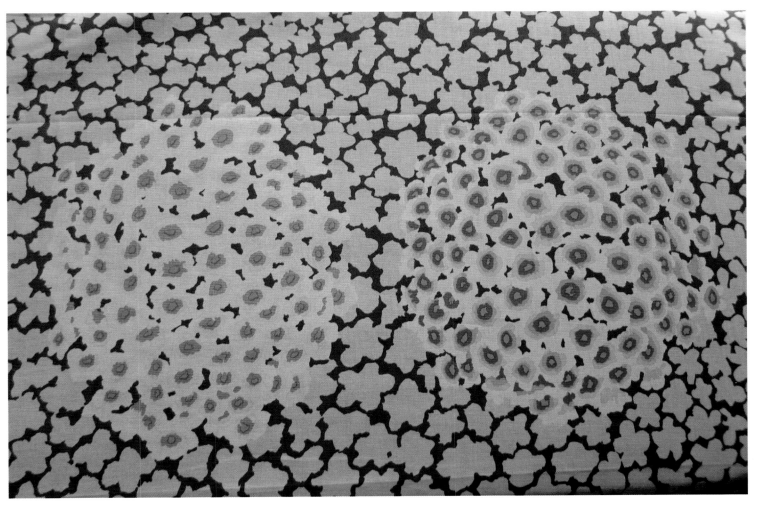

Patchwork

The moment I receive a new Kaffe Fassett Collective print collection, I sit down to dream up a series of patchwork quilt designs. I cut out the shapes I need for this new idea and place them on my flannel design wall at the end of the studio. Sometimes the idea falls into place almost immediately, but more often than not it needs a lot of editing to come right. I'll look at it through a reducing glass that condenses the colors, showing up any glaring contrasts or color-discordant notes. I remove whatever is dampening the color story and add more prints until the whole quilt starts to sing.

At this point, I photograph the new work and take the pieces down, row-by-row, to send off to a seamstress. She will receive the pieces along with the photo and start sewing the new idea together, sending me progress shots so I can go on adjusting the color balance and see that the border is appropriate.

Then, backing—usually a bold, upscale print in colors that reflect the quilt. Backing is important—in exhibitions, the audience loves to see a good bold backing. The binding is usually a small two-color print or stripe—it is like a thin ribbon that just finishes off the whole with a spicy edge.

As I have said before, most of my quilt layouts come from vintage quilts seen at festivals or in books. Every now and then, I come across a tiled floor that could be a great patchwork layout, or an abstract painting in a contemporary art museum can show me a fresh way to play with color. Even a display of beach balls or colorful umbrellas at the seaside can inspire a quilt.

I store my quilts on my attic shelves or in cupboards in my living room for easy access. They are often requested for loan to museums or quilt shops, especially when a new book comes out. The sample quilts often go to museum shows around the world. Occasionally, we sell off older quilts. When the samples are wanted for purchase, we can make a new version of it if the fabrics are still in the range. I also do special designs to feature exclusively in a magazine or for a private client. I love doing a special design for a specific room in a client's house. To pick colors and textures in my prints to enhance someone's room is an exciting challenge.

FLORAL STRIPE QUILT

In the last two or three years, I've seen a fashion print of florals on a black-and-white stripe in every variation imaginable. I spot it on T-shirts and bags mostly but have also seen it on dresses and all manner of tops. Sometimes it's big florals on bold stripes, but also sprays of delicate flowers on fine blue-and-white stripes. I'm fascinated by this persistent fashion theme because it's an idea I unleashed on the world in my 2016 book *Bold Blooms*. In that book, I showed three vases that had black-and-white stripes with roses and asters on them, so I do wonder if the world was as inspired as I am by these porcelain designs. It reminds me that, many times, a very commonly used design from a cheap child's toy or a throwaway fashion item can give me a germ of an idea that I can make my own.

I decided to use the theme for one of my latest quilts, using a smoky blue instead of black, and sprinkling an assortment of blossoms over my bold stripe base. It creates quite a fresh, springlike mood, and brings together my current obsession with two-color contrasts and my never-ending love affair with flowers.

See page 208 for detailed quilt assembly instructions.

ABOVE LEFT: My collection of striped floral vases. ABOVE RIGHT: The great Christian Lacroix in collaboration with fashion house Rixo, using the same theme on this elegant dress.

OPPOSITE: Philip Jacobs's prints that supplied fussy-cut flowers for my
Floral Stripe quilt: Dancing Dahlias, Bearded Iris, and Amaryllis.

STAMPS AND BRICKS TABLECLOTH

On my annual visit to the Houston Quilt Market in 2018, I spotted a gorgeous vintage quilt top—the black-and-cream border told me I had to have it! It's always irresistible to find a simple, doable layout that can be a good vehicle for my own prints. I had fun designing this tablecloth, as it is different from most of my quilt designs. It taps into the fascination I have with contrasting dark and light combined with color. Of course, as with many patchwork items I construct, this layout could be done in various moods: all shades of red and pinks with kick tones of emerald and turquoise would transform it; or mostly deep grays with silver and pastel lights, for instance.

See page 212 for detailed assembly instructions.

OPPOSITE: Here my Stamps and Bricks quilt hangs on my tiled garden terrace wall. A mosaic pot before it reflects the stamp section of the quilt. LEFT: The vintage quilt top that inspired my design.

RAIL FENCE QUILT

I chose this design for the book about my house because it is easy to compile, while adding up to a dynamic all-over pattern. Also, it is inspired by an antique quilt spotted on my travels, so it helps to get across how I often get inspiration from travel and the wonders of vintage quilts.

Another good point to make is the fact that I love feeding a handsome layout or motif through different mediums—I'll often do a motif in mosaic, rag rug, knitting, and needlepoint, as well as in patchwork. You can see that this rail fence pattern also works well as a knit design (on page 179), where I changed it from "on point" to straight on, to make it an easier knit project.

What intrigues me about this vintage quilt is the use of gently shading prints, done so scrappily that it's not obvious at first. It's amazing how ending each block of brick shapes in black pulls the otherwise quite random blocks into a distinct rail fence pattern.

See page 216 for detailed quilt assembly instructions.

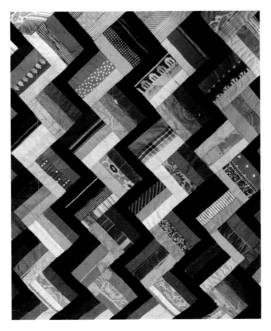 

OPPOSITE: My Rail Fence quilt glows in my dining room with mosaic garden pieces next to it. ABOVE LEFT: The vintage quilt that led to my Rail Fence quilt. ABOVE RIGHT: Rail Fence quilt detail.

Needlepoint

There is something quite alluring about an image made up of fragmented bits—beaded bags where flowers and landscapes are depicted in a grid of glass beads, Roman mosaics, and images in parks made up of decorative flower beds all delight and fascinate me. Likewise, needlepoint is pictures made from a grid of stitches in colored wools.

The task I give myself is to try to make a multicolored needlepoint cushion cover in as few colors as possible. I used to limit myself to twelve shades, but these days I go to as many as twenty or so if it's a limited-edition kit and larger than a cushion. I keep my needlepoint yarns in big plastic tubs divided by color groups: reds, pinks, and oranges in one; blues, lavenders, and turquoises in another; multi-greens in one; yellows, grays, and whites in another; and, last, a large collection of autumnal browns, golds, and rusts.

First, I find my image—sometimes a composition of several flowers, or shapes formed in art books or magazines. I draw them out on paper to get the right scale and proportion, then I trace this image onto my canvas leaving a 2-inch (5-cm) border all around (so I can stretch the finished work back into shape—stitching can distort the canvas). I use waterproof pen to draw on the canvas so that I can dampen it later for stretching without the ink running.

I start to stitch right away with a carefully selected group of yarns. I often pick colors a little too light (to my eye), because the colors seem to darken slightly when stitched. Each stitch has a depth of shadow around it that makes the color look deeper. I tend to jump around the canvas, trying a leaf here, a flower there, and a bit of background, to see how each color affects its neighbor. The completed design is an image made up of a mosaic of wool stitches, which pleases me. The most important aspect of everything I do is color harmony and enhancement.

The stitched canvas alongside the color sketch I did when starting my Radish cushion project.

I took up needlepoint after a few years of knitting, as it allowed me to work on more detailed subject matter. Knit designs are usually geometrics or simplified florals, so they can be easily knitted in a more limited pallet. Needlepoint encouraged me to stitch faces, realistic flowers, and vegetables (my favorite).

Stitching on a canvas is very nearly as contemplative and addictive as knitting. Again, it's very difficult to put down until you have completed that flower . . . now let's see how it looks surrounded by the background color . . . and now let's see how that leaf settles in behind that big bloom, and so on.

ABOVE: Tracing my artwork onto a canvas to stitch a tapestry of medieval buildings. OPPOSITE: Cats, frogs, and poppies in my cushion pile in the living room.

ABOVE: Painting out the artwork for my Enchanted floral print fabric. BELOW: Stitching a needlepoint idea from the finished artwork. OPPOSITE: This design is a study of circular forms in a rosy palette, available from Ehrman Tapestry.

My Chechnyan rug that inspired my "Villanelle" needlepoint cushion, which is now
a kit from Ehrman Tapestry.

BLOOD RED ROSE ON BLUE CUSHION

Through the years, I've done many studies of single flowers in needlepoint. Usually, they are in the bright sunlight tones that I hope go with bright, modern, white-walled surroundings. Because I also have a love of dark, mysterious color combinations, I decided to stitch a rose in the deepest maroon palette and place it on a dark teal ground. I love the burnt orange and pink edges and little glints of light at the center of the opened rose. It reminds me of "The Nightingale and the Rose," the Oscar Wilde story of the bird that pierces her heart to turn a white rose to a crimson one. This would be handsome on a black leather couch or chair, or a rich jewel accent in a moss green or cloud gray room.

See page 224 for the chart and instructions.

ABOVE LEFT: My first drawing for Blood Red Rose. I traced this onto canvas and started stitching.

ABOVE RIGHT: I often love the way the partially stitched design looks—a little like a jigsaw puzzle.

GOLD STRIPED TULIP CUSHION

Stripes have always attracted me, but lately I'm seeing how they cut through the other patterns life presents to us: a man in a bold two-color striped robe in a crowded Afghani market; an arch of contrasting stone stripes always seems celebratory to me; circus tents and awning stripes feel the same. I love the old photos of football clubs—all those striped jerseys gathered in a group. When stripes occur in nature, it always catches my eye. The reference for this striped tulip was cream and dark maroon, but I fancied the boldness of police-tape yellow and black. My black here is really a dark prune color, but it reads as black against that blast of golden yellow. The striped background has a rich depth that throws the flower forward.

See page 226 for the chart and instructions.

RADISH CUSHION

The older I get, the more beauty I see in humble vegetable forms. The cheeky contrasting colors of this radish begged to be portrayed in this miniature needlepoint. Making something on this intimate scale is great fun after the large scale I often work on in quilts or knitted shawls and coats. I used my Aboriginal Dot print to border the needlepoint.

See page 228 for the chart and instructions.

Knitting

Of all the main disciplines I employ, knitting is the most centering and therapeutic. When I cast on and start to build a pattern (I never preplan my colors in patterned knitting), I feel a warm tingle and sense of adventure. It's the same thrill I used to get as a boy wandering into a canyon in Big Sur for the first time, sensing I was going to encounter a beautiful undiscovered world. The actual physical act of knitting is already so mysterious—you rub two sticks together with yarn and out comes this magic web of color.

I usually start by spotting an idea on a carpet or pattern detail of a mosaic in a magazine—some geometric motif or stylized flower that I can see will be translatable to knitting stitches. I will draw that idea in little symbols onto graph paper and start to knit in any contrasting colors, just to manifest the idea in knitted form. It is very important to then put that first swatch up on my design wall and view it from a distance. If it catches my eye several times in the next day or so, I know it's good enough to develop.

Then, the real creativity kicks in, as I gather a palette of colored yarns to develop the motif into a viable design. I might create a few different partial color swatches until I feel the colors really sing when seen from across the room. At that point, I will cast on a hundred or so stitches and start knitting a scarf, throw, shawl, or the back of a garment. As I knit, the colors may change as I adjust my vision of the piece, so that a repeat pattern will have variations as it grows into my ideal level of contrast and harmony. The process of actually knitting these motifs is always deeply satisfying and difficult to bring to a pause, even for lunch.

As I arrive at my finished combinations of tones in the patterns, I think of the ways you knitters out there will make this idea your own. It's exciting to feel that some knitters will change the scale of the motif or take part of it to make a border, and definitely introduce their own color mood. It's a great thrill for me to see how a knitter has used the bare bones of my idea to make a very personal statement.

ABOVE: A garment designed for Peruvian Connection's catalog, for which I do two collections a year.
OPPOSITE: A knitted patchwork of bright swatches, all in strong geometric themes.

Knitting on my corner chair, using circular needles to create this checkerboard
throw in a dusty palette.

ABOVE: A swatch of tweedy knitting that almost disappears on my worn carpet.
OPPOSITE: A patchwork of knitted swatches from various projects, all in a very
neutral palette.

RAIL FENCE KNIT

On our travels to the States, Brandon and I once came across a vintage patchwork that really moved me. It had a bold overall zigzag design that snagged our attention. When I looked closer, I could see the layout was made up of simple blocks—four "bricks" of color going from light to dark. Each block ended with a black "brick," which created a rail fence effect. I loved the simplicity of the blocks that added up to such a strong overall impression.

When I came to knit this design, I noticed the quilt was "on point," meaning that all the square blocks were tilted diagonally. That would have made for quite a complicated knit, but doing the blocks straight on was easier to reproduce, so that's what I decided to do. I feel it's more doable, but the effect is still dynamic.

At first, I repeated the color groups in regular progression, so that green, red, blue, then gray blocks followed each other in a predictable pattern. Somehow, this lacked the charming randomness of the quilt, so I started being more random, and I much preferred the results. You will see that at first I kept to the same greens, reds, blues, and lavenders in my blocks, but as the piece progressed I started ringing the changes—bringing in different shades of those colors, so the blocks look the same at first glance but are subtly different as the piece progresses. This is something I observe in many intricate textiles, such as carpets and embroideries from the Middle East, and is what, for me, makes them so wonderfully rich and imaginative—the changes in symmetry and repeat patterns make the work so much more alive.

If you like the effect of the same blocks repeated, that's fine—just stick to the first few rows of blocks that I completed in my piece, then repeat the same collection of colors throughout your piece. If you prefer the random feel, just use your stash of colors to improvise changes as you progress up the great zigzag pattern. Always end each block with a dark brick and you will keep the rail fence profile going. You might also notice that I started with black as my dark, then changed to deep navy for most of the throw.

For colors and knitting chart, see page 232.

ABOVE: The first swatch testing colors and layout for the Rail Fence throw.

TUMBLING BLOCK THROW

I first noticed the tumbling-block pattern on the tiled footpaths leading up to the doors of London houses, and the three-dimensional effect intrigued me. I first knitted up the pattern in the late 1960s, when I was working on my first book, *Glorious Knitting*. Knitting it was a delight. You cast on stitches in multiples of twenty, so each block starts with one stitch in a dark color, eighteen stitches in a medium color, and one stitch in a pale color. You then knit ten rows, increasing the dark and light diamonds until they meet. Knitting six more rows has you ready to introduce the next medium-colored "top" to your blocks.

At first, I changed all the colors constantly, so I'd have several light tones, a range of medium tones, and several dark sides to the blocks. Then, looking at vintage patchwork quilt books, I noticed that old tumbling-block patterns often kept the dark sides of the blocks to one shade of dark brown or black. This made it a more cohesive design and a little easier to knit. It's so easy to memorize the layout and concentrate on your color palette that it becomes quite addictive to take on as a project. Although I've done countless variations on the design, I can't see it ever being any less of a favorite.

For this lap blanket, I used the colors of my Chinese ancestral portrait to inspire my dusky palette. I used Rowan's sparkling range of Felted Tweed, including the colors I helped design. I also doubled the yarn, so the motifs are brought up in scale and it makes a warmer blanket. Best of all, it's faster to knit. Make it any size you fancy, either by adding blocks or a larger border. A garter stitch border in wide stripes would help it to lie flatter as a blanket.

For colors and knitting chart, see page 234.

ABOVE: Tumbling Blocks throw, close-up. OPPOSITE: Checking the colors against my
Chinese ancestral portrait, which inspired my palette.

MARBLE SNOWBALL

On a trip to Italy, Brandon took a photo of a marble mosaic floor (page 189), and I now include it in my slideshow for my lectures about color. Every time it is shown and I talk about this floor, I am reinspired to make something using these subtle colors and the crisp black-and-white checkerboard. In fact, combining black and white elements with color has been a recent obsession of mine. For the past few years, I've done a number of patchwork textile prints using contrast tones behind floral and leaf prints. I've also used it in quilts and in my knits for Peruvian Connection and Rowan.

When I cast on to make this stole, I picked the softest, most neutral tones from the Rowan Felted Tweed range, along with the darkest gray (Seafarer 170), and off-white for the checkerboards. I introduced lavender, peach, and sweet pink to lift the pales a little, while keeping it all very soft and stone-like.

I rang the changes in color combinations for ten snowball rows of the pattern, then started repeating the same color sequence, but arranging the proportions of the colors differently. You can use the same colors, but feel free to arrange the quantities of each one as you feel. This way, the design does not have an obvious repeat.

Any of the knits in this book can be used in whatever way your imagination pictures them. This design could be a man's waistcoat, a long sleeveless jacket for a woman, a set of cushions, or you could double up the yarns and make a cozy blanket in any size, from cot to king. I look forward to seeing pictures of wherever your creativity takes you.

For colors and knitting chart, see page 236.

ABOVE: The shining marble floor in St Mark's Cathedral, Venice, that inspired my knitted throw.

Painting

The first lesson I learned as a painter was to sharpen up my drawing. As a figurative painter, drawing was the structure that supported my colors. A wonderful Scandinavian sous chef in my parents' restaurant was an exquisite draftswoman—we were all entranced by her witty drawings. One day, she advised the preadolescent me to draw the things I saw every day—even if it was only my own hand, a coffee cup, or a folded napkin. Hand-eye coordination was to be cultivated. A very cogent lesson.

Another good lesson came to me when I had the good fortune to go to a wonderful boarding school where the arts were encouraged. My art teacher was watching me draw one day and uttered the words that became a magic formula for my future drawing: "When drawing an object, try to keep your pen on the page uninterrupted for as long as possible." This single piece of advice made me look much more intently at whatever I was trying to draw, and to make a few simple lines define the subject, rather than the hesitant little scratches I had used until then.

Another artist gifted me with advice when I was about to take flight in my career. "An artist has only two morals to uphold: get up early in the morning, and keep your brushes clean." Since discipline was always a scary subject for me, convinced I had none and that it was painfully hard to acquire, this was just enough to keep me going. Later, I learned that discipline, in the activity that rewards you, comes more and more easily as you feel the benefits of constant trying.

The first thing I do when starting a still life is to arrange my objects on a surface with good directional light. I try to make good color arrangements, so that the painting has a color story. The French painter Bonnard said, "A painting is first and foremost an arrangement of colors."

The next step, after arranging my objects, is to draw them out on my canvas, at first in a light color such as yellow ochre or light blue. Once drawn, I study the composition and start to adjust certain aspects. Perhaps the whole group is too high on the canvas, leaving an empty void at the bottom, or the pieces are drawn too large or too small. With a more definite color, such as red or dark blue, I'll re-draw the arrangement.

Next, I start filling in color. A wash of color for the background and foreground quickly sets the objects in a definite space. Then, if the objects are a deepish color, I start filling in tones that give me any overall perception of the tonal composition. If there are a lot of white-based objects, I paint soft gray shadows on each pot with the idea of painting patterns on them later in the process. So, at first, these pale vases look like a black-and-white photograph.

I constantly put the painting up on the wall in my textile studio next door, so I can study it from a distance. Layer upon layer of colors brings the work more and more alive. The difficulty here is to go further with the painting than at first feels necessary. As I stare at the work in the next-door studio, I sort of finish it in my mind and feel no need to go further. Yet further work always seems to more satisfyingly tell whatever color story I'm aiming for. It's my task to bring the inner vision to the surface of a work, so viewers can more clearly see what I see.

We all know what it's like to see a play or film that remains a mystery to us because the playwright or filmmaker didn't go far enough to share his or her vision with us. When I sell a painting and come across it sometime later on the buyer's wall, I'm always grateful for the extra work I put in to communicate. Sometimes I don't even recognize it as my work at first. Just the slight thrill that a painting makes a clear lively impression is reward enough for the time spent making it.

TOP: Painting in my sister Holly's house in Big Sur, California. BOTTOM: Painting in London.

Still life of a patchwork quilt with Victorian kitchen items (owned by Liza Prior Lucy).

OPPOSITE: My favorite ginger jars—they remind me of my mother, who loved all Chinese objects.
ABOVE: Finished painting of the ginger jars on a Guatemalan embroidery with artichokes from our garden.

OPPOSITE: A still life set-up using green, turquoise, and blue pots. TOP: Starting the painting on a "painted over" canvas, filling in my drawing with white paint. BELOW: Adding gray shadows and the start of the blue striped background.

The finished still life.

It has been a great pleasure to show off the color laboratory that this house has become over the fifty years I have lived here. Since there is so much history here, I have decided to leave the house intact to prosperity, full of the collections of treasures from our travels and creative output. The next generation of makers and designers, or just souls in need of a color fix, will be able to come and see where it all originated. Meanwhile, I hope this "virtual" tour on paper has inspired you to use color and pattern in your own personal way.

Part Three

HOW TO

FLORAL STRIPE QUILT

The quilt is made up of a background of alternating strips in Fabrics 1 and 2, with borders in the same fabrics. Flowers in Fabrics 3, 4, 5, and 6 are backed with double-sided fusible webbing, fussy cut and appliquéd to the background.

FINISHED SIZE

64 × 82½ inches (163 × 210 cm)

NOTE

¾ yard (70 cm) each of Fabrics 3, 4, 5, and 6 will be more than enough to cut 50 flowers. Regardless of where the repeat falls on the fabric, it is possible to cut about 70 flowers, so you will have plenty of choice in which flowers to use.

FABRICS

Quilt Top

Fabric 1	Aboriginal Dot	Cream	PWGP071	2¾ yards (2.6 m)
Fabric 2	Shot Cotton	Airforce	SCGP104	2⅛ yards (2 m)
Fabric 3	Amaryllis	Natural	PWPJ104	¾ yard (70 cm)
Fabric 4	Cactus Flower	Multi	PWPJ096	¾ yard (70 cm)
Fabric 5	Bearded Iris	Cool	PWPJ105	¾ yard (70 cm)
Fabric 6	Dancing Dahlias	Multi	PWPJ101	¾ yard (70 cm)

Backing

| Fabric 7 | Paper Fans | Delft–Backing | PWGP143 | 5⅛ yards (4.7 m) |

Binding

| Fabric 8 | Aboriginal Dot | Iris–Binding | PWGP071 | ⅝ yard (60 cm) |

Batting

72 × 91 inch (183 × 231 cm) single piece

Other supplies

| Double-sided fusible webbing for flower appliqués | | 2 yards (1.9 m) |

CUTTING OUT

Fabric requirements are calculated at a maximum width of 40 inches (102 cm) and are cut across the width of the fabric, unless otherwise stated.

Background and Borders

From Fabric 1, cut 26 strips, each 3½ × 40 inches (8.9 × 102 cm).

From Fabric 2, cut 23 strips, each 3 × 40 inches (7.6 × 102 cm).

Remove selvages and, using a ¼ inch (6 mm) seam allowance, sew the strips end to end to make a long strip in each fabric.

Cut the following pieces from the fabric strips (if you find a fabric join sits very close to the beginning of a piece, cut off the join before measuring and cutting the piece):

Fabric 1

8 pieces: 60½ × 3½ inches (153.7 × 8.9 cm) for quilt center.
2 pieces: 65½ × 3½ inches (166.4 × 8.9 cm) for round 1 sides.
2 pieces: 53 × 3½ inches (134.6 × 8.9 cm) for round 1 top and bottom.
2 pieces: 76½ × 3½ inches (194.3 × 8.9 cm) for round 3 sides.
2 pieces: 64 × 3½ inches (167.6 × 8.9 cm) for round 3 top and bottom.

Fabric 2

9 pieces: 60½ × 3 inches (153.7 × 7.6 cm) for quilt center.
2 pieces: 47 × 3 inches (119.4 × 7.6 cm) for center top and bottom.
2 pieces: 71½ × 3 inches (181.6 × 7.6 cm) for round 2 sides.
2 pieces: 58 × 3 inches (147.3 × 7.6 cm) for round 2 top and bottom.

Appliqué Flowers

From Fabrics 3, 4, 5, and 6, select the flowers to be appliquéd. Allowing approximately a ¼ inch (6 mm) border around the outside of each flower, iron fusible webbing to the back of each one (follow the manufacturer's instructions). If two flowers are very close together, apply fusible webbing as a single item. With small sharp scissors, carefully cut out each flower around the outlined edges. Repeat until you have around 50 flowers cut from the 4 fabrics.

Backing

Cut Fabric 7 into 2 equal lengths, remove selvages, and sew the 2 pieces together. Trim to 72 × 91 inches (183 × 231 cm).

Binding

From Fabric 8, cut 8 strips, each 2½ inches (6.4 cm) wide. Remove selvages and sew end to end.

ASSEMBLY DIAGRAM

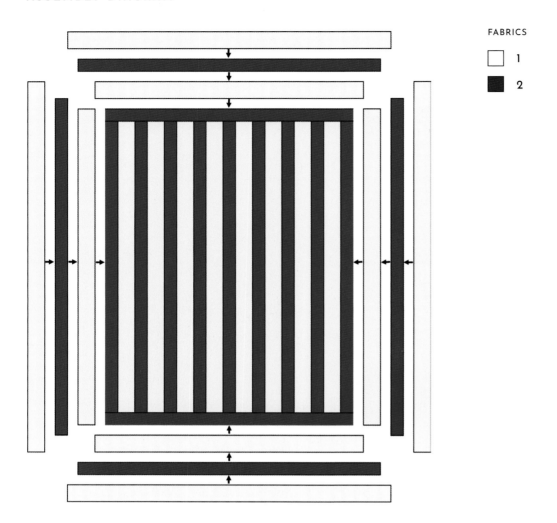

FABRICS

☐ 1

■ 2

MAKING THE BACKGROUND

Use a ¼ inch (6 mm) seam allowance throughout.

Quilt Center

Referring to the Assembly Diagram, pin and sew alternating strips of Fabrics 1 and 2 together (pieces measuring 60½ inches/153.7 cm long), starting and finishing with a Fabric 2 piece. To prevent bowing and stretching the long pieces, turn the piece around and pin each strip in place before sewing from alternating ends. Together, the 17 strips will make a piece 47 × 60½ inches (119.4 × 153.7 cm). Press the seams toward the darker fabric. Pin and sew the center top and bottom Fabric 2 pieces (measuring 47 × 3 inches/119.4 × 7.6 cm) to the top and bottom of the striped block to complete the quilt center.

Border

For each round, join the longer side pieces before the shorter top and bottom pieces. Always pin the pieces together before sewing and press all seams toward the darker fabric after adding each set.

Round 1

Sew the Fabric 1 pieces (65½ × 3½ inches/166.4 × 8.9 cm) to each side.
Sew the Fabric 1 pieces (53 × 3½ inches/134.6 × 8.9 cm) to the top and bottom.

Round 2

Sew the Fabric 2 pieces (71½ × 3 inches/181.6 × 7.6 cm) to each side.
Sew the Fabric 2 pieces (58 × 3 inches/147.3 × 7.6 cm) to the top and bottom.

Round 3

Sew the Fabric 1 pieces (76½ × 3½ inches/194.3 × 8.9 cm) to each side.
Sew the Fabric 1 pieces (64 × 3½ inches/167.6 × 8.9 cm) to the top and bottom.

FLOWER APPLIQUÉ

Arrange the flowers in the chosen positions, referring to the quilt photograph and Flower Placement Diagram, if required. Apply flowers to the background by removing the backing paper and fusing in place according to the fusible web manufacturer's instructions.

Appliqué the edges by machine, using either a narrow zigzag stitch or a stitch of your choice.

Once you have stitched your appliqué, carefully cut away the background fabric from the wrong side of the fabric, to within ¼ inch (6 mm) of the appliqué stitching. This keeps the fabric from becoming too bulky and keeps the color of the background from showing through.

FLOWER PLACEMENT DIAGRAM

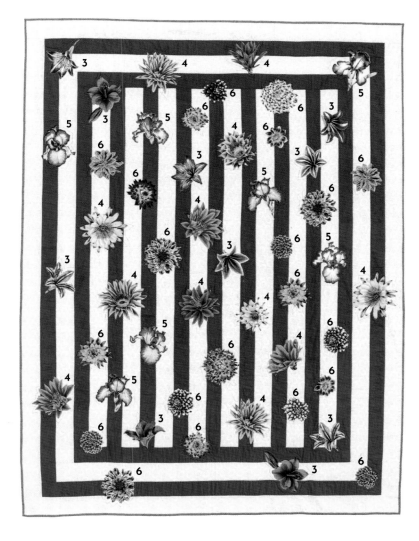

Fabric 3: Amaryllis

Fabric 4: Cactus Flower

Fabric 5: Bearded Iris

Fabric 6: Dancing Dahlias

FINISHING THE QUILT

Press the quilt top and backing. Layer the quilt top, batting, and backing, then baste the layers together (see page 223).

Quilt in the ditch along the stripes and echo quilt around the flowers.

Trim the quilt edges. Press the binding strip in half and sew onto the quilt edges (see page 223).

STAMPS AND BRICKS TABLECLOTH

On one of my trips to the Houston Quilt Market, I came across an intriguing patchwork of small squares and bricklike rectangles. What drew me to it was the blast of color in simple forms surrounded by a bold black-and-cream border. Somehow, all those sharp colors were so well balanced by the strong contrasting frame. It has no batting, so it is perhaps meant to be a tablecloth. I set to work doing a version of it in sharper, fresher colors and ended up with a work very different from my usual romantic tonal designs. I could see this in a room with a black-and-white checkerboard floor and white walls, with a great bowl of oranges and a brilliant contrasting flower arrangement sitting on it.

FINISHED SIZE
74½ × 74½ inches (189 × 189 cm)

THE BLOCKS
The center panel is made up of 5 rows, each containing 5 nine-patch blocks. Each finished nine-patch block measures 6 inches (15.2 cm) square, and is constructed of 2½ inch (6.4 cm) squares, finished 2 inch (5.1 cm) square, in 2 alternating layouts. Refer to the Block Assembly Diagram.

The brick border is made up of 9 concentric rounds of bricks, each cut 8½ × 2½ inches (21.6 × 6.4 cm) and finished at 8 × 2 inches (20.3 × 5.1 cm).

The outer border is made up of alternating squares and contrasting smaller bricks. The squares are cut 2½ inches (6.4 cm) square and finished at 2 inches (5.1 cm) square. The bricks are cut 6½ × 2½ inches (16.5 × 6.4 cm) and finished at 6 × 2 inches (15.2 × 5.1 cm).

FABRICS

Top

Fabric 1	Spot	Duck Egg	GP70DE	¼ yard (25 cm)
Fabric 2	Spot	Pond	GP70PO	⅜ yard (40 cm)
Fabric 3	Spot	Ochre	GP70OC	½ yard (50 cm)
Fabric 4	Spot	Silver	GP70SV	⅝ yard (60 cm)
Fabric 5	Spot	Noir	GP70	⅜ yard (40 cm)
Fabric 6	Spot	Sapphire	GP70SP	⅜ yard (40 cm)
Fabric 7	Spot	White	GP70WH	¼ yard (25 cm)
Fabric 8	Aboriginal Dot	Ocean	GP71ON	¼ yard (25 cm)
Fabric 9	Aboriginal Dot	Red	GP71RD	⅜ yard (40 cm)
Fabric 10	Aboriginal Dot	Shocking	GP71SG	½ yard (50 cm)
Fabric 11	Shot Cotton	Pistachio	SSGP111	⅜ yard (40 cm)
Fabric 12	Shot Cotton	Aubergine	SSGP117AB	1⅝ yards (150 cm)
Fabric 13	Shot Cotton	Opal	SSGP114	¾ yard (70 cm)
Fabric 14	Shot Stripe	Cantaloupe	SCGP001	⅛ yard (15 cm)
Fabric 15	Jumble	Rose	BM53	¼ yard (25 cm)
Fabric 16	Jumble	Tangerine	BM53TN	¼ yard (25 cm)
Fabric 17	Jumble	Turquoise	BM53TQ	¼ yard (25 cm)
Fabric 18	Mad Plaid	Contrast	BM37CO	¼ yard (25 cm)
Fabric 19	Mad Plaid	Maroon	BM37	¼ yard (25 cm)
Fabric 20	Roman Glass	Lavender	GP01LV	¼ yard (25 cm)
Fabric 21	Guinea Flower	White	GP51WH	¼ yard (25 cm)

Backing

Fabric 22	Fruit Mandala*	Pink	QBGP00PK	2¼ yards (210 cm)

*108 inches (274 cm) wide backing fabric

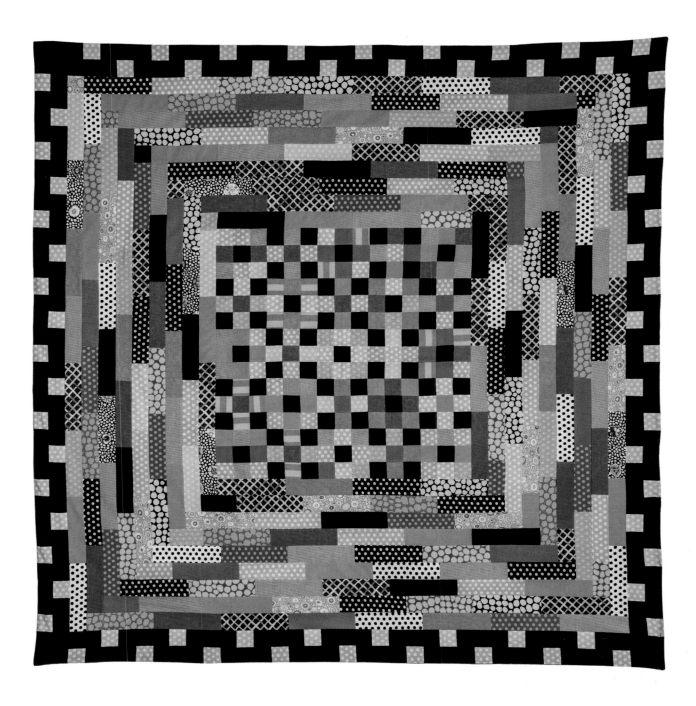

CUTTING OUT

Fabric requirements are calculated at a maximum width of 40 inches (102 cm). All pieces are cut from 2½ inch (6.4 cm) strips, cut across the width of the fabric. You can cut the following number of pieces from each strip:

2½ inch (6.4 cm) squares	16 per strip	293 in total
8½ × 2½ inch (21.6 × 6.4 cm) bricks	4 per strip	229 in total
6½ × 2½ inch (16.5 × 6.4 cm) small bricks	6 per strip	75 in total

Cut 2½ inch (6.4 cm) strips from fabrics and cross cut pieces as follows:

		Center	Brick Border	Outer Border
Fabric 1:	2 strips	7 squares	4 bricks	
Fabric 2:	4 strips	15 squares	10 bricks	
Fabric 3:	6 strips	24 squares	16 bricks	
Fabric 4:	7 strips	21 squares	4 bricks	68 squares
Fabric 5:	5 strips		18 bricks	
Fabric 6:	4 strips		13 bricks	
Fabric 7:	3 strips		12 bricks	
Fabric 8:	3 strips	12 squares	8 bricks	
Fabric 9:	5 strips	16 squares	14 bricks	
Fabric 10:	6 strips	17 squares	17 bricks	
Fabric 11:	4 strips	15 squares	10 bricks	
Fabric 12:	21 strips	61 squares	16 bricks	75 small bricks
Fabric 13:	6 strips	22 squares	16 bricks	
Fabric 14:	1 strip	15 squares		
Fabric 15:	3 strips		10 bricks	
Fabric 16:	3 strips		10 bricks	
Fabric 17:	3 strips		10 bricks	
Fabric 18:	3 strips		11 bricks	
Fabric 19:	3 strips		12 bricks	
Fabric 20:	3 strips		11 bricks	
Fabric 21:	2 strips		7 bricks	

Backing
Trim Fabric 22 to 74½ × 74½ inches (189 × 189 cm)

MAKING THE BLOCKS

Make 25 nine-patch blocks using the photograph and Block Assembly Diagram for patch placements. Lay out the 9 squares and sew them together in 3 rows of 3. Press the seams in alternating directions for each row, then sew the 3 rows together.

The nine-patch blocks alternate between 2 different layouts as shown in the Block Assembly Diagram:

Block A: nine-patch block with 4 corner squares in Fabric 12—make 12.
Block B: nine-patch block with 1 central square in Fabric 12—make 13.

BLOCK ASSEMBLY DIAGRAM

Block A   Block B

CENTER DIAGRAM

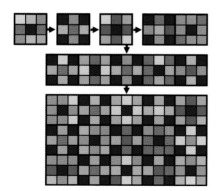

ASSEMBLING THE TABLECLOTH

Use a ¼ inch (6 mm) seam allowance throughout.

Center Panel
On a design wall, lay out the 25 nine-patch blocks as shown in the photograph or Center Diagram, or lay out as you prefer in 5 rows of 5 blocks. Sew the blocks together into rows, press, and sew the 5 rows together.

ASSEMBLY DIAGRAM

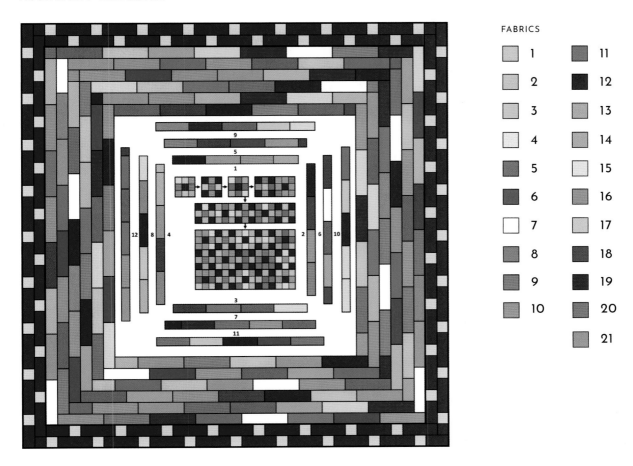

FABRICS

▢	1	▢	11
▢	2	▢	12
▢	3	▢	13
▢	4	▢	14
▢	5	▢	15
▢	6	▢	16
▢	7	▢	17
▢	8	▢	18
▢	9	▢	19
▢	10	▢	20
		▢	21

Brick Border

Following the Assembly Diagram, sew enough bricks together for each round, working from left to right. On several rounds the last piece on the right-hand side will need to be trimmed down to either 2½ inches (6.4 cm), 4½ inches (11.4 cm), or 6½ inches (16.5 cm) to fit the previous round.

Work around the tablecloth in a clockwise direction, starting at the top, sewing strips of bricks onto the center panel, round by round, until you have added all 9 rounds.

Outer Border

The outer border is made up of 2 rows of alternating small bricks and blocks. The dark bricks in Fabric 12 alternate with contrasting squares in Fabric 4. Refer to the photograph. Arrange the blocks around the tablecloth on a design wall and construct in the same way as the brick border.

FINISHING THE TABLECLOTH

Press the top and backing pieces, place and pin the right sides together. Starting away from a corner, stitch the 2 layers together around the edge, leaving a generous ¼ inch (6 mm) seam allowance, and stop sewing to leave an opening 6 inches (15.2 cm) from your starting point. Trim the corners and turn the tablecloth right side out through the opening, using a blunt rounded object to push out the corners from the inside. Blind stitch the opening and press the tablecloth.

Hand quilt around the tablecloth center to anchor the two fabric layers.

RAIL FENCE QUILT

This is a variation on a traditional Rail Fence quilt. I was inspired by an antique quilt (shown on page 155) made in this pattern and set on point. I decided to make my own pepped-up version in the latest collection of Kaffe Fassett Collective fabrics.

FINISHED SIZE

64 × 83 inches (163 × 211 cm)

THE BLOCKS

Blocks are squares formed of 4 rectangular "bricks" set in a dark to light color order: dark, medium-dark, medium-light, and light. Each finished brick measures 2 × 8 inches (5.1 × 20.4 cm); together they form 8 × 8 inch (20.4 × 20.4 cm) finished squares. Each block is made using Fabric 1 and three other fabrics graded in color groups. Blocks are set on point in alternating directions, with the dark bricks of Fabric 1 creating strong zigzag lines down the quilt.

Side setting and corner blocks are made the same way, then trimmed using Template A for the side setting triangles and Template B for the top and bottom left-hand corners.

FABRICS

Quilt top

Fabric 1	Wide Stripe	Ink	SSGP001	1¾ yards (1.7 m)
Fabric 2	Shot Cotton	Paprika	SCGP101	¼ yard (25 cm)
Fabric 3	Shot Cotton	Pistachio	SCGP111	⅜ yard (40 cm)
Fabric 4	Shot Cotton	Lupin	SCGP113	¼ yard (25 cm)
Fabric 5	Shot Cotton	Pimento	SCGP116	¼ yard (25 cm)
Fabric 6	Shot Cotton	Heliotrope	SCGP106	⅜ yard (40 cm)
Fabric 7	Shot Cotton	Harissa	SCGP115	¼ yard (25 cm)
Fabric 8	Shot Cotton	Opal	SCGP114	⅛ yard (15 cm)
Fabric 9	Jumble	Magenta	PWBM053	⅜ yard (40 cm)
Fabric 10	Jumble	Saffron	PWBM053	¼ yard (25 cm)
Fabric 11	Jumble	Turquoise	PWBM053	⅜ yard (40 cm)
Fabric 12	Jumble	Maroon	PWBM053	¼ yard (25 cm)
Fabric 13	Flower Dot	Purple	PMBM077	⅜ yard (40 cm)
Fabric 14	Flower Dot	Warm	PMBM077	⅜ yard (40 cm)
Fabric 15	Flower Dot	Aqua	PWBM077	¼ yard (25 cm)
Fabric 16	Spot	Sapphire	PWGP070	¼ yard (25 cm)
Fabric 17	Spot	Mauve	PWGP070	¼ yard (25 cm)
Fabric 18	Millefiore	Gray	PWGP092	⅛ yard (15 cm)
Fabric 19	Millefiore	Mauve	PWGP092	⅜ yard (40 cm)
Fabric 20	Roman Glass	Lavender	PWGP001	¼ yard (25 cm)
Fabric 21	Watermelons	Blue	PWPJ103	¼ yard (25 cm)
Fabric 22	Octopus	Turquoise	PWBM074	⅜ yard (40 cm)
Fabric 23	Agate	Blue	PWPJ106	¼ yard (25 cm)
Fabric 24	Stream	Orange	PWBM075	⅜ yard (40 cm)
Fabric 25	Animal	Orange	PWBM076	¼ yard (25 cm)

Backing

Fabric 26	Oranges	PWGP177	Purple	5¼ yards (4.9 m)

Binding

Fabric 27	Spot	PWGP070	Purple	⅝ yard (60 cm)

Batting

72 × 91 inch (183 × 231 cm) single piece

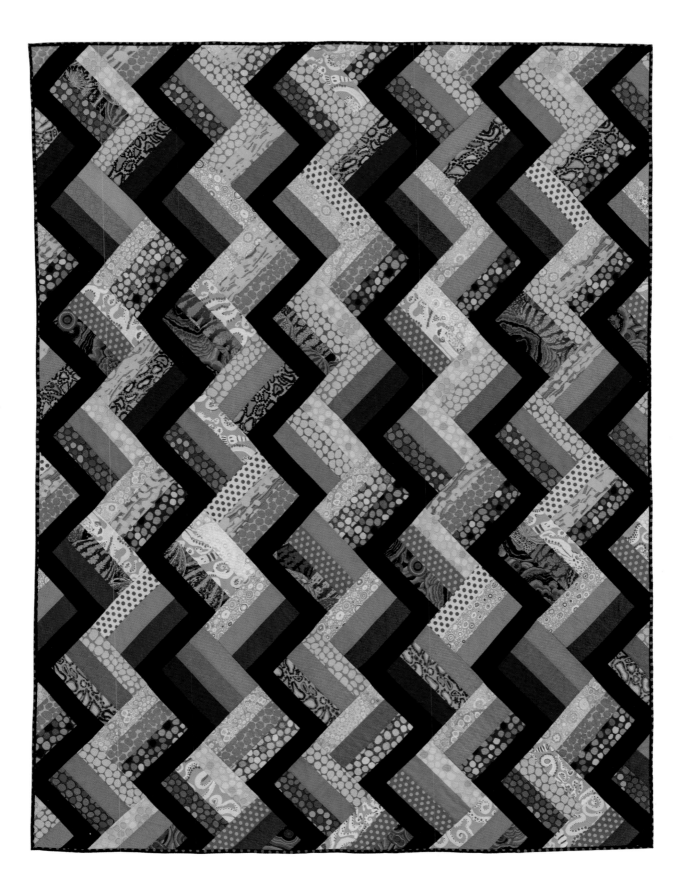

CUTTING OUT

Fabric requirements are calculated at a maximum width of 40 inches (102 cm) and are cut across the width, unless otherwise stated. Cut strips 2½ inches (6.4 cm) wide and cross cut bricks 2½ × 8½ inches (6.4 × 21.6 cm). You will be able to cut 4 bricks from each strip. Cut fabrics and cross cut as follows:

Fabric 1: 23 strips–90 bricks

Fabric 2: 3 strips–12 bricks

Fabric 3: 4 strips–14 bricks

Fabric 4: 3 strips–11 bricks

Fabric 5: 3 strips–10 bricks

Fabric 6: 4 strips–13 bricks

Fabric 7: 2 strips–8 bricks

Fabric 8: 1 strip–2 bricks

Fabric 9: 4 strips–13 bricks

Fabric 10: 3 strips–11 bricks

Fabric 11: 4 strips–14 bricks

Fabric 12: 2 strips–5 bricks

Fabric 13: 4 strips–15 bricks

Fabric 14: 5 strips–20 bricks
(includes 5 bricks used wrong side up)

Fabric 15: 3 strips–11 bricks

Fabric 16: 3 strips–10 bricks

Fabric 17: 2 strips–7 bricks

Fabric 18: 1 strip–3 bricks

Fabric 19: 5 strips–19 bricks

Fabric 20: 2 strips–8 bricks

Fabric 21: 2 strips–8 bricks

Fabric 22: 4 strips–15 bricks

Fabric 23: 3 strips–10 bricks

Fabric 24: 4 strips–16 bricks

Fabric 25: 3 strips–12 bricks

Backing

Cut fabric 26 into 2 equal lengths, remove selvages, and sew together along the side seam. Trim backing to 72 × 91 inches (183 × 231 cm).

Binding

From fabric 27, cut 8 strips, each 2½ inches (6.4 cm) wide. Remove selvages and sew together end to end.

MAKING THE BLOCKS

Blocks are made in 5 different color groups: pink, green, orange, mauve, and blue, each with variations in fabrics used.

Select a brick of Fabric 1, along with a medium-dark, a medium-light, and a light fabric in the same color group and sew them together as shown in the Block Assembly Diagram. Make 6 blocks for each row in the same color, using different fabrics in the same color group. (Or, if you prefer, copy the blocks in my original.) You will need 15 sets of 6 blocks to make up the rows of the quilt, 90 blocks in total: 4 rows in pink, 3 rows in green, 3 rows in orange, 2 rows in mauve, and 3 rows in blue. Note that some of the pink blocks include Fabric 14 used wrong side up to achieve a lighter version of the fabric (refer to the quilt photograph).

BLOCK ASSEMBLY DIAGRAM

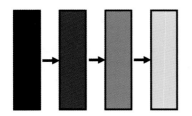 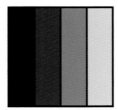

QUILT ASSEMBLY

Following the Quilt Assembly Diagram for placement of the blocks, lay the blocks out on a design wall forming 15 rows on point, ensuring your blocks are positioned correctly. Stand back and check that you are happy with the arrangement of colors.

Once happy with the overall look, use Template A (Side Setting Triangle) to cut the sides, top, and bottom blocks into setting triangles. Use Template B (Corner Triangle) to cut the left top and bottom blocks to the correct size. Take care to position the template over the section you want to keep, then cut and discard the excess. It is important to note that the setting triangles will leave bias edges on the outside edge of the quilt, so handle these with care. Spray with starch and stay stitch the long side of the triangles as you make them to avoid distorting the quilt edges when sewn together.

Sew the blocks into diagonal rows as shown in the Quilt Assembly Diagram, then sew the rows together to complete the quilt top.

QUILT ASSEMBLY DIAGRAM

FINISHING THE QUILT

Press the quilt top and backing and layer the quilt top, batting, and backing, then baste the layers together (see page 223).

Quilt in the ditch around each block or in your preferred design.

Trim the quilt edges. Press the binding strip in half and sew onto the quilt edges (see page 223).

TEMPLATES

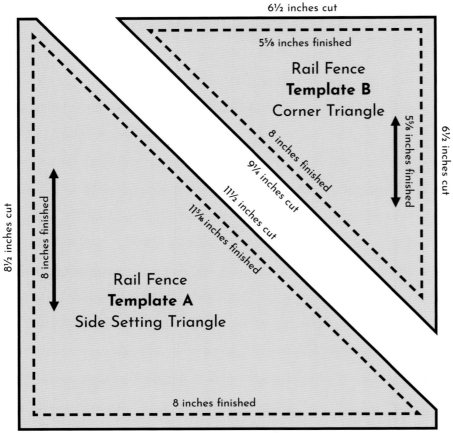

Enlarge templates by 200% to achieve the correct size. The dashed lines represent the sewing lines, and the solid lines represent the cutting lines. The arrows indicate the direction of the fabric grain.

QUILTING BASICS

This chapter isn't designed to cover all the various quilting shortcuts, but the tips provided here will make the quilt-making process easier and more fun. Don't get too worried about technique at first. Concentrate instead on the beautiful colors you are using and on composing them into a spectacular quilt.

PATCHWORK FABRICS

The best materials to use are the lightweight, 100 percent cotton fabrics that are specially produced for quilt-making. As they are firmly woven, they are easy to cut, crease, and press, but slow to fray.

Choosing fabric colors and prints

The fabrics used for the quilts in this book are from the Kaffe Fassett Collective. Feel free to select your own color palette instead of the ones suggested. The most fun part of patchwork, I believe, is playing with and mixing fabric colors and finding a palette that really sings!

Always look carefully at the photograph of the quilt when choosing your fabric palette. Choose prints with care. Notice the scale of the prints. Very small-scale prints can look like solids at a distance, but they provide more interest and visual "texture" than solids. Large-scale floral prints are particularly useful because you can cut completely different colors from different areas of the same fabric. Dots and stripes, even used in only a few areas of a quilt, add amazing movement to the composition.

When choosing multicolored prints, study them at a distance. Looking at them up close, you may think you are choosing a particular color, but at a distance they turn into something completely different. For example, you may think you are choosing a "red" because there are bright red small-scale motifs on a white ground, but at a distance it looks pink! Similarly, motifs in two different colors will blend together at a distance to make a new color. Separate blues and yellows on the same print will make it look green.

If in any doubt, buy small amounts of fabrics and test them by cutting and arranging some patches and then standing back to see the effect at a distance.

Determining how much fabric you need

Deciding on fabric amounts for my designs is not a very exact science, because I use so many different fabrics. The quantities in the instructions tend to be generous. It is better to have too much fabric than too little, and you can use the leftovers for future projects.

If you do run out of fabric, don't look on it as a tragedy. Think of it as a design opportunity! The replacement you find may make the quilt look even better. After all, quilt making was a craft designed to use up scraps, and chance fabric combinations sometimes resulted in masterpieces.

When calculating exact fabric amounts for borders, bindings, or backings, remember that although specially made cotton patchwork fabrics are usually 44 inches (112 cm) wide, the usable width is sometimes only 40 inches (101.5 cm) due to shrinkage and the removal of selvages.

Preparing patchwork fabric

Prewash your fabrics before use, especially if they are vintage. This will confirm colorfastness and preshrink the fabric in case it may be prone to this. Wash darks and lights separately and rinse them well. Press with a hot iron while still damp. After pressing, cut off the selvages.

TOOLS AND EQUIPMENT

Aside from a sewing machine, you'll need:

- fabric scissors
- pins
- needles
- ruler
- lead and chalk pencils
- tape measure
- ironing board and iron
- template plastic
- rotary cutter
- cutting mat
- an assortment of rotary-cutting rulers

Template plastic is perfect for making durable and precise shapes to trace around. The rotary cutting tools will help you cut your patches quickly and in accurate straight lines. Having a range of large and small cutting mats and rotary-cutting rulers is handy, but if you want to start out with just one of each, buy a 12 × 18 inch (30 × 46 cm) mat and a 6 × 12 inch (15 × 30 cm) ruler. The ruler will have measurement markings on it, as well as 90°, 60°, and 45° angles.

Design wall and reducing glass

The other two items I strongly recommend for successful patchwork are a design wall and a reducing glass. A full-size quilt can be arranged on the floor, but it is much easier to view when on a wall. My design wall is large enough for a queen-size bed cover and is made with two sheets of insulation board, each measuring 4 × 8 feet (122 × 244 cm). Any sturdy, lightweight board would do, but insulation board is handy, as it can be cut with a craft knife.

To make a design wall, cover one side of each of the boards with a good-quality cotton flannel in a neutral color. I have designed the ideal flannel for this purpose—it is light gray and has printed on it a pale-colored 2-inch (5-cm) grid. The grid helps me align my quilt pieces on the wall and gives me an instant idea of the size of the pieces. Join the boards with three "hinges" of sticky tape so they can be folded and put away.

A quilter's reducing glass looks like a magnifying glass, but instead of making things look larger, it makes them look smaller. By looking at a fabric or a design in progress through a reducing glass, you can see how the fabric print or even a whole patchwork layout will look at a distance. This makes the errors in color or pattern in the design pop out and become very obvious. Reducing glasses are usually available in shops that sell patchwork supplies. A camera isn't quite as good but is an acceptable substitute.

PATCH PREPARATION

Once you have prepared all the fabrics for your patchwork, you are ready to start cutting patches. Squares, rectangles, and triangles can be cut quickly and accurately with a rotary cutter, but you will need to use scissors for more complicated shapes.

Using a rotary cutter

Always use the cutter in conjunction with a cutting mat and a rotary-cutting ruler. Press down on the ruler and the cutter and roll the cutter away from you along the edge of the ruler. With a little practice, you will be able to cut patches very quickly. Long strips can be cut from folded fabric, squares from long strips, and half-square triangles from squares.

Making templates

Photocopy templates to the size you need and cut them out before you begin your quilt. If the shapes can be cut quickly with a rotary cutter, use the template as a guide to your rotary cutting. If not, you can make a plastic or cardboard template from them and use it to trace around.

SEWING PATCHES TOGETHER

The quilt instructions each feature a layout diagram for how to arrange the various patch shapes to form the quilt design. Often, several patches are joined together to form small blocks and then the finished blocks are sewn together to form the whole quilt. Whether arranging a block or a whole quilt, lay the patches out on the floor or on a design wall. Then, study the effect of your arrangement, stepping back to look at it or looking at it through a reducing glass.

Stitch pieces together only once you are sure the color arrangement is just right. Remember that an unpredictable arrangement will have more energy and life than one that follows a strict light/dark geometry.

Machine-stitching straight seams

Sew, or piece, patches together using a ¼ inch (6 mm) seam allowance and following the order specified in the quilt instructions. Use the same neutral-colored thread to piece the entire patchwork. I find that medium taupe or gray thread will work for most patchworks. But when the overall palette is very light, use ecru thread.

Pin the patches together with right sides facing and match the seam lines and corner points carefully. (If you are proficient at the sewing machine, you will be able to stitch small squares together without pinning.) Always stitch from raw edge to raw edge. There is no need to work back-stitches at the beginning and end of each patch seam.

To save time and thread, you can chain-piece the patches. To do this, feed through the paired together pieces one after another without lifting the presser foot; the machine will stitch through nothing a few times before it reaches the next pair of patches. Simply clip the pairs of patches apart when you're finished.

Pressing seams

Press all seams flat first, to embed the stitches. Then, open out the patches and press the seam allowances to one side, or press open if many fabrics meet in one spot (to reduce bulk). As you continue stitching patches into blocks, then the blocks into rows as instructed, press the seam allowances in each row (of patches or blocks) in the same direction. Press the seam allowances in every alternate row in the opposite direction to avoid having to stitch through two layers of seam allowances at once when joining the rows together.

APPLIQUÉ

One of the quilts in this book uses appliqué, which is the addition of shaped fabric pieces on top of a backing fabric. The raw edges of the appliqué motifs are covered with machine stitching or can be hand-stitched if you prefer.

Cut the shapes from well-pressed fabric with sharp scissors. If you are using machine blanket, buttonhole, or satin stitch to cover the raw edges of the appliqué and secure it to the backing, pin or baste the shapes in place first.

After stitching, carefully cut away the backing fabric behind the appliqué to within ¼ inch (6 mm) of the seam to keep the fabric from becoming too bulky.

QUILTING AND FINISHING

After you have finished piecing your patchwork, press it carefully. It is now ready to be quilted.

Preparing the quilt backing and batting

Choose a backing fabric that will not do a disservice to the quilt top—they ought to have a certain charm of their own and go well with the patchwork top. Cut the selvages off the backing fabric, then seam the pieces together to form a backing at least 4 inches (10 cm) bigger all around than the patchwork top.

Batting comes in various thicknesses. I prefer to use thin 100 percent cotton batting, as it gives a quilt the attractive, relatively flat appearance of an antique patchwork. Unroll the batting and let it rest before cutting it to about the same size as the backing.

Basting together the quilt layers

To keep the layers of the quilt firmly in place during the quilting process, baste them together or use safety pins to secure all three layers. Lay the backing wrong side up and place the batting on top of it. Lay the finished, pressed patchwork right side up on top of the batting.

Beginning at the center for each stitching line, baste stitch or pin two diagonal lines from corner to corner through the layers of the quilt. Work stitches about 3 inches (7.5 cm) long and try not to lift the layers too much as you stitch or pin. Next, always beginning at the center and working outward, baste horizontal and vertical lines about 4 inches (10 cm) apart across the layers.

Choosing a quilting pattern

I love to hand quilt. Simple parallel rows of stitches are my preferred pattern, as I like quilting that does not overshadow the play of the patchwork fabrics. For this reason, when my quilts are machine quilted I often choose stitch-in-the-ditch quilting. In this type of quilting, the stitching lines are worked very close to the patch seams and are invisible on the right side of the quilt. Echo quilting is another simple quilting pattern that suits many patchwork designs. It is worked by stitching ¼ inch (6 mm) inside the patch seam lines to echo the shape of the patch. A third favorite machine quilting pattern is outlining motifs on large-scale prints, such as individual flowers, with quilting stitches.

Choose a suitable quilting thread color—it should ideally blend invisibly into the overall color of the patchwork quilt when it is viewed from a distance.

Binding quilt edges

Remove the basting (tacking) threads that held the layers together. Then, trim away the excess batting and backing right up to the edge of the patchwork, straightening the edge at the same time, if necessary.

Cut binding strips either on the bias or on the straight grain of the fabric, 2–2½ inches (5–6 cm) wide. To make a strip long enough to fit around the edge of the quilt, sew these strips together end-to-end, joining bias strips with diagonal seams. Next, fold the strip in half lengthwise with the wrong sides together and press.

Place the doubled binding on the right side of the quilt, with the right sides facing and the raw edges of both layers of the binding aligned with the raw edges of the quilt. Machine stitch ¼ inch (6 mm) from the edge and stitch up to ¼ inch (6 mm) from the first corner. Make a few backstitches and cut the thread ends. With the edge just stitched at the top, fold the binding upward so that it makes a 45° angle at the corner of the quilt. Keeping the diagonal fold just made in place, fold the binding back down and align the edges with the next side of the quilt. Beginning ¼ inch (6 mm) from the top and side of the corner, stitch down the next side to within ¼ inch (6 mm) of the next corner, and so on. When you reach the beginning of the binding, turn under the edge of one end and tuck the other end inside it.

Finally, turn the folded edge of the binding to the back of the quilt and hand stitch it in place, folding a miter at each corner.

BLOOD RED ROSE ON BLUE CUSHION

Deep, dark palettes of jewel colors have a special place in my heart. This mysterious, dark rose seems to glow on its teal background. The few spots of paler color at its center seem to accentuate the burnt darkness of the bloom. It's so at home on my blue velvet chair.

FINISHED SIZE

The finished needlepoint measures 16 inches (40.6 cm) wide by 16 inches (40.6 cm) tall.

MATERIALS NEEDED

- 10-stitches-to-the-inch (2.5 cm) interlock needlepoint canvas, 20 inches (50.8 cm) square
- Appleton wool tapestry yarn (11 yard/10 m skeins) in 11 colors (see below)
- Size 18 tapestry needle
- ½ yard (50 cm) of a 44-inch (112-cm) wide cotton fabric, for backing, and matching sewing thread
- 2 yards (1.9 m) of ready-made decorative cord (optional), for edging
- Pillow form to fit finished cover

YARN COLORS AND AMOUNTS

716	Wine Red	5 skeins
505	Scarlet	6 skeins
504	Scarlet	9 skeins
501A	Scarlet	1 skein
226	Bright Terra Cotta	2 skeins
946	Bright Rose Pink	2 skeins
944	Bright Rose Pink	1 skein
751	Rose Pink	1 skein
696	Honeysuckle Yellow	1 skein
474	Autumn Yellow	1 skein
487	Kingfisher	15 skeins

EMBROIDERY NOTES

The chart is 161 stitches wide by 161 stitches tall. Follow the chart using tent stitch and one strand of yarn. Fill in the background last. See page 230 for basic needlepoint and finishing instructions.

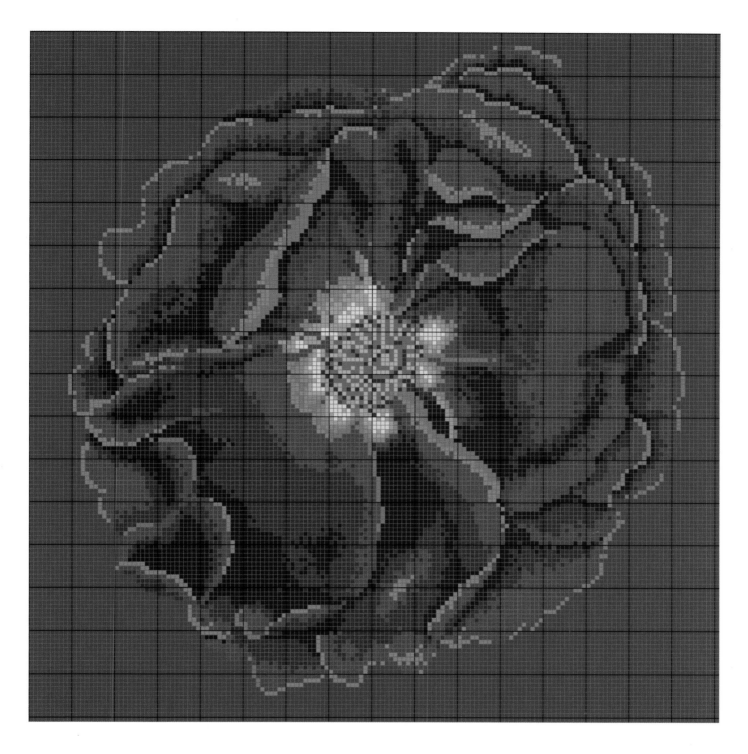

KEY

■ 716   ■ 504   ■ 226   ▨ 944   ■ 696   ■ 487

■ 505   ■ 501A   ■ 946   ▢ 751   ▨ 474

GOLD STRIPED TULIP CUSHION

I've always loved stripes, but in the past few years I've grown obsessive about layering stripes on stripes. This tulip with almost-black maroon, hot gold, and scarlet touches is one of nature's strongest stripe stories. I put it on a tonal striped ground to further my stripe-on-stripe story.

FINISHED SIZE

The finished needlepoint measures 16½ in (42 cm) wide by 16½ in (42 cm) tall.

MATERIALS NEEDED

- 10-stitches-to-the-inch (2.5 cm) interlock needlepoint canvas, 20½ in (52 cm) square
- Appleton wool tapestry yarn (11 yard/10 m skeins) in 10 colors (see below)
- Size 18 tapestry needle
- ½ yard (50 cm) of a 44-in (112-cm) wide cotton fabric, for backing, and matching sewing thread
- 2 yards (1.9 m) of ready-made decorative cord (optional), for edging
- Pillow form to fit finished cover

YARN COLORS AND MOUNTS

474	Autumn Yellow	7 skeins
553	Bright Yellow	6 skeins
935	Dull Mauve	8 skeins
505	Scarlet	1 skein
502	Scarlet	2 skein
643	Peacock Blue	1 skein
402	Sea Green	1 skein
297	Jacobean Green	7 skeins
454	Bright Mauve	10 skeins
501A	Scarlet	3 skeins

EMBROIDERY NOTES

The chart is 163 stitches wide by 164 stitches tall. Follow the chart using tent stitch and one strand of yarn. See page 230 for basic needlepoint and finishing instructions.

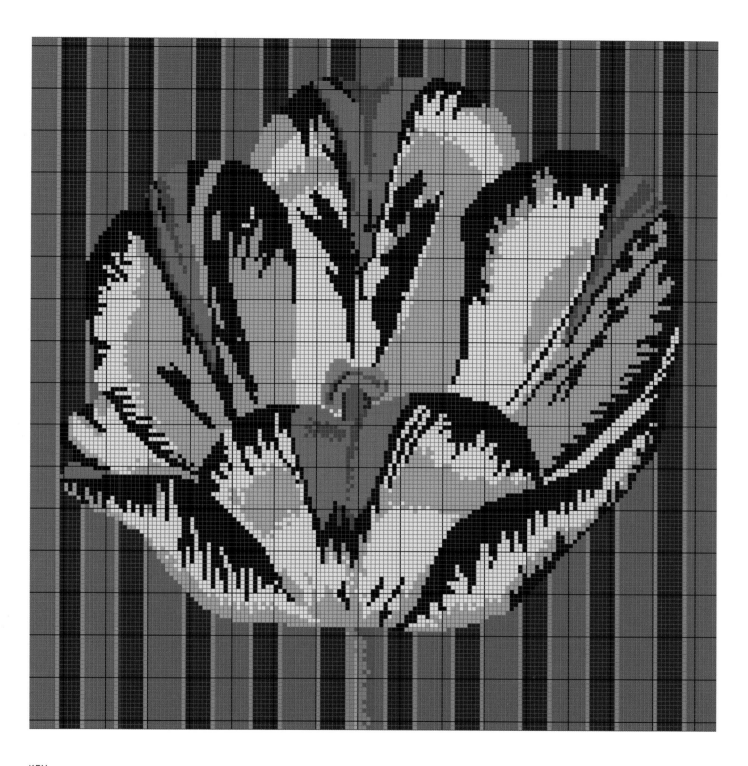

KEY

474	935	502	402	454
553	505	643	297	945

RADISH CUSHION

The leafy world of vegetables is such a natural subject for needlepoint. This radish, with its contrasting tones of white and deep pink, gives this vegetable portrait a real bit of zest. I made it small, so you can mount it as the center of a cushion with a print or damask surround. Perhaps add a border of a pretty patterned ribbon, too.

FINISHED SIZE

The finished needlepoint measures 11 inches (28 cm) wide by 11½ inches (29.2 cm) tall.

MATERIALS NEEDED

- 10-stitches-to-the-inch (2.5 cm) interlock needlepoint canvas, 15½ inches (39.3 cm) square
- Appleton wool tapestry yarn (11 yard/10 m skeins) in 11 colors (see below)
- Size 18 tapestry needle
- ½ yard (50 cm) of a 44-inch (112-cm) wide cotton fabric, for backing, and matching sewing thread
- 1⅓ yards (1.2 m) of ready-made decorative cord (optional), for edging
- Pillow form to fit finished cover

YARN COLORS AND AMOUNTS

254	Grass Green	1 skein
251	Grass Green	1 skein
253	Grass Green	1 skein
474	Autumn Yellow	7 skeins
561	Sky Blue	4 skeins
421	Leaf Green	4 skeins
944	Bright Rose Pink	1 skein
946	Bright Rose Pink	3 skeins
948	Bright Rose Pink	1 skein
992	Off White	1 skein
963	Iron Gray	1 skein

EMBROIDERY NOTES

The chart is 110 stitches wide by 114 stitches tall. Follow the chart using tent stitch and one strand of yarn. See page 230 for basic needlepoint and finishing instructions.

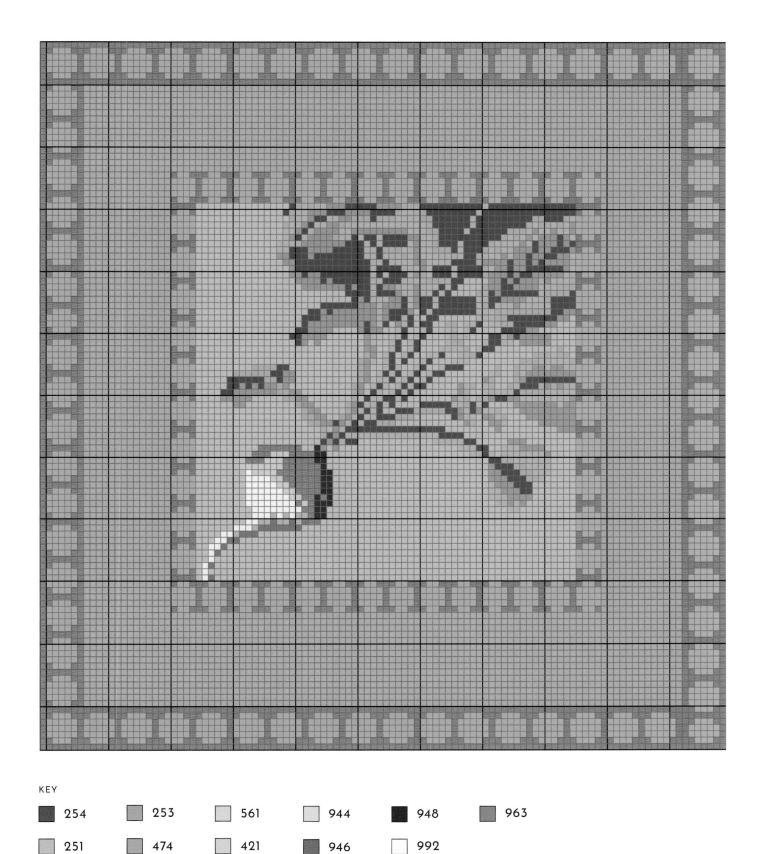

KEY

■	254	■	253	▦	561	▦	944	■	948	▦	963
■	251	■	474	▦	421	■	946	▦	992		

NEEDLEPOINT BASICS

BUYING CANVAS AND YARNS

Use the recommended canvas. The amount of canvas specified in the instructions is enough to leave about 3 inches (7.5 cm) extra all around the design. If you like, you can purchase slightly less, but it is best to have a minimum of 2 inches (5 cm) of unworked canvas all around the edge to make blocking easier.

Although it may be possible to use substitute tapestry-weight yarns for the recommended yarns, it is best to use the brand and shade numbers I have specified if you want to duplicate my design exactly. The amounts listed for the yarns are on the generous side but are only approximate. It is not possible to be absolutely sure that they will be adequate for every single stitcher, as amounts needed can vary based on how loosely or tightly the stitches are worked.

EMBROIDERING THE DESIGN

Begin by marking the outline of the design on your canvas and, if desired, dividing it into tens just like the charted design, using a fabric marker pen. Note that each canvas intersection represents a stitch. Following the chart, work the embroidery in tent stitch (see below), using one strand of wool tapestry yarn.

Tent stitch

The simplest stitch to work, this small, diagonal stitch crosses over the intersection of one horizontal (weft) and one vertical (warp) thread of the canvas. This forms a slanted stitch at a 45° angle.

BLOCKING AND SIZING

You may find that your needlepoint looks slightly distorted as stitching progresses. Do not worry about this; the wool yarns can be blocked into shape after the stitching is completed.

To block the finished needlepoint, place it facedown on a flat surface and dampen it lightly using a damp cloth or sponge. Place the needlepoint facedown on a large sheet of plywood. Begin nailing it to the plywood, stretching it out to approximately the finished measurements given in the instructions. Start with a tack in the center of each of the four sides of the needlepoint, nailing into the unworked canvas. Then add tacks from the center outward toward the corners, spacing them about 1 inch (2.5 cm) apart.

Leave the needlepoint to dry completely, even if it takes several days. I then use wallpaper paste as a "size" to fix the shape. Mix the wallpaper paste to a fairly thick consistency. With the needlepoint still nailed in place, brush a light film of paste into the back. Remove only when completely dry.

MAKING THE CUSHION BACK

Each set of needlepoint instructions tells you how much fabric you will need to make a back for your cushion. Although you can insert a zipper into the cover, it is easiest to create an "envelope" back. An envelope back consists of two panels of fabric that overlap at the center. Then, a pillow form can be inserted or removed through the open overlap.

To make the back, after you have blocked your needlepoint, trim the empty canvas around the embroidery to ¾ inch (2 cm). This is the seam allowance. Next, measure the size of the canvas in both directions. Each back panel should measure half the size of these measurements, plus an extension of 3 inches (7.5 cm) along the center (overlapping) edge.

After calculating the size of the back panels, cut out the two pieces. Fold and press ½ inch (12 mm) to the wrong side along the center (overlapping) edge of one piece, then press under ½ inch (12 mm) again to create a double hem. Machine-stitch the hem in place. Finish the center edge of the other panel in the same way.

Next, lay the needlepoint faceup on a flat surface. Lay the back panels facedown on top of the needlepoint with the hemmed edges overlapping at the center and the raw edges aligned with the raw edges of the canvas. Pin and baste stitch (tack) the back panels in place. With the needlepoint uppermost, machine-stitch close to the embroidery all around the edge. If you are sewing on a decorative cord, leave a ½ inch (12 mm) opening in the seam in the center of the bottom edge.

Trim the seam allowance to ½ inch (12 mm) and clip off the corners diagonally about ¼ inch (6 mm) from the seam. Turn the cover right side out.

Finally, if using, sew on the decorative cord along the seam line, tucking the ends into the small opening in the seam.

RAIL FENCE KNIT

YARNS

I used Rowan Felted Tweed and started with the following colors:

Dark bricks: Black 211; changing to Seafarer 170 farther up the piece.
Brown block: Scarlet 222; Barn Red 196; Phantom 153.
Green block: Vaseline Green 204; Avocado 161; Lotus Leaf 205.
Red block: Heliotrope 219; Peony 183; Rage 150.
Blue block: Fjord 218; Turquoise 202; Ultramarine 214.
Gray block: Scree 165; Delft 194; Carbon 159.
Pink block: Frozen 185; Barbara 200; Barn Red 196.
Lavender block: Astor 217; Iris 201; Seasalter 178.
Orange block: Mineral 181; Zinnia 198; Barn Red 196.

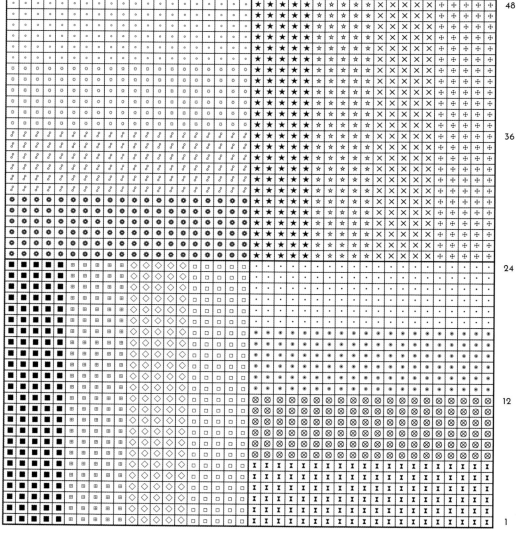

rep = 40 stitches (x 48 rows)

TUMBLING BLOCK THROW

YARNS

Use the colors listed to make your own blocks. Always use black as the dark side of the blocks, one of the lights for the light sides, and one of the mediums for the top of the blocks. Sometimes, the same color can be used as a medium or a light. I used Rowan Felted Tweed.

rep = 20 stitches (x 48 rows)

Lights	
165	Scree
173	Duck Egg
181	Mineral
183	Peony
190	Stone
200	Barbara
201	Iris
203	Electric Green
204	Vaseline Green
212	Peach
213	Lime
215	Ciel
216	French Mustard
217	Astor
222	Scarlet

Mediums	
145	Treacle
150	Rage
153	Phantom
154	Ginger
172	Ancient
175	Cinnamon
178	Seasalter
183	Peony
186	Tawny
196	Barn Red
200	Barbara
201	Iris
202	Turquoise
205	Lotus Leaf
215	Ultramarine

Darks	
211	Black

MARBLE SNOWBALL

The knitter will see that each "snowball" in this design uses two or three colors of Rowan Felted Tweed in a very marble-like palette. Consult the line drawing to see which colors are used in each snowball. I've not spelled out exactly how many rows of each of the three tones to use—that is left to you. If you adore grays and want a predominance of gray tones in your knit, make the gray shades in each combination the majority tone.

You will notice that I've given combinations for the first 10 rows of snowballs. Then, repeat from the bottom row through the first 10 rows. If you use the combinations differently, the repeat will not be obvious. You will soon be knitting on your own without having to consult the chart, as the pattern is easy to memorize—just count the rows up each snowball before starting the next one. The checkerboard sections of the layout are the same throughout.

If you wanted a completely different effect from my soft marble palette, try a really dark, rich story with jewel tones and black and a deep color for your checkerboards. Alternatively, try a bright pastel palette for a spring-like effect.

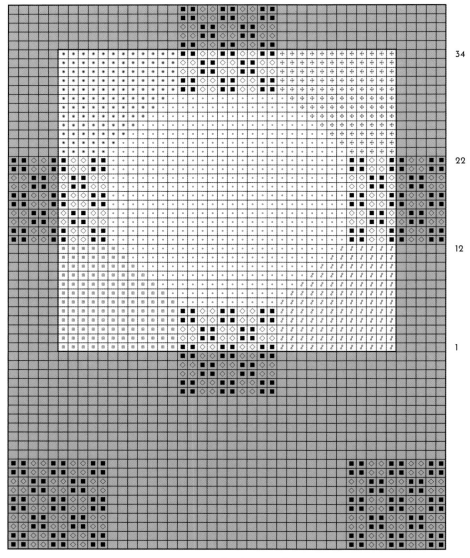

rep = 34 stitches (x 34 rows)

YARNS

152	Watery
154	Ginger
157	Camel
165	Scree
172	Ancient
173	Duck Egg
175	Cinnamon
177	Clay
178	Seasalter
184	Celadon
185	Frozen
190	Stone
191	Granite
211	Black
212	Peach
216	French Mustard
217	Astor
218	Fjord
219	Heliotrope

SNOWBALL YARN COMBINATIONS

1   Duck Egg 173 / Granite 191 / Fjord 218
2   Camel 157 / Cinnamon 175 / Frozen 185
3   Scree 165 / Celadon 184
4   Cinnamon 175 / Ginger 154 / Ancient 172
5   French Mustard 216 / Celadon 184
6   Peach 212 / Camel 157 / Frozen 185
7   Fjord 218 / Watery 152 / Astor 217
8   Watery 152 / Ancient 172 / Duck Egg 173
9   Cinnamon 175 / Ginger 154 / Peach 212
10 Cinnamon 175 / French Mustard 216 / Celadon 184
11 Watery 152 / Ancient 172 / Seasalter 178
12 Frozen 185 / Celadon 184 / Camel 157
13 Duck Egg 173 / Heliotrope 219 / Astor 217
14 French Mustard 216 / Stone 190 / Celadon 185
15 Peach 212 / Camel 157 / Frozen 185
16 Duck Egg 173 / Celadon 184
17 Astor 217 / Duck Egg 173 / Heliotrope 219
18 Celadon 184 / Fjord 218
19 Heliotrope 219 / Frozen 185 / Camel 157
20 Watery 152 / Duck Egg 173 / Ancient 172
21 Fjord 218 / Watery 152 / Duck Egg 173
22 Frozen 185 / Heliotrope 219 / Peach 212
23 French Mustard 216 / Cinnamon 175 / Celadon 184
24 Cinnamon 175 / French Mustard 216 / Celadon 184
25 Peach 212 / Camel 157
26 Ancient 172 / Celadon 184 / Watery 152
27 Camel 157 / Frozen 185 / Heliotrope 219
28 Astor 217 / Duck Egg 173 / Granite 191
29 Cinnamon 175 / Peach 212 / Watery 152
30 Heliotrope 219 / Frozen 185 / Granite 191
31 Granite 191 / Fjord 218 / Watery 152
32 Frozen 185 / Camel 157 / Heliotrope 219
33 Stone 190 / Celadon 184 / Granite 191
34 Fjord 218 / Camel 157 / Granite 191
35 Watery 152 / Fjord 218 / Scree 165

Checkerboards: Black 211 and Clay 177